Presented to

....

On the Occasion of

....

Date

....

Currents of the Heart

Glimpses of God in the Stream of Life

Gigi Graham Tchividjian

FAMILY
CHRISTIAN
PRESS

CURRENTS OF THE HEART
Published by Multnomah Publishers, Inc.

©1996 by Gigi Graham Tchividjian.
International Standard Book Number: 0-88070-933-2
Special FCP Edition: 1-893065-28-6

Cover illustrations by Robin Molin/Conrad Represents
Cover designed by Kirk DouPonce

Printed in the United States of America

Unless otherwise noted, Scripture quotations are from: The Holy Bible, New International Version (NIV) ©1973, 1984 by International Bible Society, used by permission of Zondervan Publishing House

Also quoted: The New King James Version (NKJV) ©1984 by Thomas Nelson, Inc.
The King James Version (KJV)
The Living Bible (TLB) ©1971 by Tyndale House Publishers
The Amplified Bible (TAB) ©1965 by Zondervan Publishing House.

FOR INFORMATION:
MULTNOMAH PUBLISHERS, INC.
POST OFFICE BOX 1720
SISTERS, OREGON 97759

99 00 01 02 03 04 — 7 6 5 4 3 2 1

This book is lovingly dedicated to all my daughters:

Berdjette, Jerushah,
Lisa, Lydia, and Kimberly.

Each of them is a source of joy and inspiration to me
as I observe them trusting God in the
currents of their lives.

∽

"The *daughter's* heart is in the hand of the LORD,
like rivers of water;
he turneth it whithersoever he will."

-KING SOLOMON

CONTENTS

Ripples in the Stream

Rapids and Whirlpools

Quiet Pools

IN APPRECIATION...

A book is not written alone.

In my case, it takes a patient, understanding husband and family. And mine has once again proven to be a source of encouragement to me.

It takes a good, very sensitive editor, not only one who appreciates my work, but ideally is also a friend. I have the privilege of working with the best...Larry Libby. Without you, I would have given up.

It takes faithful friends like Les Troyer and Steve Griffith to iron out all the wrinkles, offer encouragement, and see that the job is done right.

Sometimes it takes the help of freelance editors. For this project, Sue Ann Jones took the challenge, and because of her gentle touch on my manuscript, my mind and my nerves were calmed and we were able to meet the deadlines.

It takes a talented art and graphic design department. This one had to go back to the drawing board at the last minute. Thank you, David Uttley, for designing and putting together a finished product of which we can all be proud.

It takes many others who answer the phones, send the FedEx packs, write the letters, market, do publicity and countless other behind-the-scenes jobs. Most of you I do not know by name, but I appreciate you all.

And finally, it takes a publisher who believes in me and is willing to pull all of its resources together, put its name on the book, and then see that it is available to the readers. This is our third project together, and I value our relationship.

Each of you has experienced the currents of birthing a book. Without you, this would not have been published.

So, simply from my heart...thank you!

INTRODUCTION

Behind my childhood home in the mountains of North Carolina, a stream bubbles and chatters year round.

I can't calculate how many hours I spent on its banks, watching for crawdads, salamanders, and minnows, wading in its merry current, peeking under the rocks, or dreaming at the edge of its pools. Sometimes as I waded, a crawfish would lift his bright orange or deep brown claw and warn me away from his dwelling with a pinch. At other times, I would spy a bright object flashing suddenly through the water. Reaching down, I might claim a piece of gleaming mica, a tiny garnet, or other semi-precious stone. With a bit of luck, I might even lift out a real ruby.

In the same way, I believe, the Lord brings sudden insights into the flow and tumble of everyday life. Someone once defined an insight as "a sudden glimpse of the obvious." You might call it a new way of seeing something that has been there all along. Like a precious stone under the water, it may lie there for months and years...until it suddenly catches a particular angle of sunlight—and flashes like fire.

I'd like to say these glimpses occur every time I kneel in prayer or step into a church. But that wouldn't be true. Instead they come like flashes from a streambed...at unexpected moments...while I'm building a brick walkway, flying a kite, lying in bed unable to sleep, fixing dinner, gazing through an airliner window, watching my son drive away, wiping away a tear, or playing with the children in the sand. The Lord gives me an insight, a sudden glimpse of the obvious, that adds depth to my spirit and gives me a greater understanding of the many riches He provides to His children.

The meditations on the following pages have not been arranged in anything approaching chronological order. Christmas musings may fall before Thanksgiving essays, and summer writings juxtapose with wintry thoughts. Yet they do have an order...they're arranged according to the "currents" in which they flow.

First come the ripples, the gentle little waves that give our lives form and texture, occurring over and over again, fluid yet constant patterns that push us along from morning to night. Perhaps it is while we are in this mundane, involuntary current of ripples, bobbling along day after day, that our spiritual glimpses are the most unexpected.

Next come the rapids and whirlpools—insights gained during challenges faced and lessons learned. These are the currents we may ride with fear, frustration, anger, or broken hearts, either plunging over the ragged edge of despair or circling endlessly in monotony...until we remember to reach for help and find Him always there, His hand outstretched to lift us up.

And finally come the sparkling pools, the easy, peaceful currents in which we grow and rest and look for depth in the quiet moments of our lives.

It is through these small glimpses of God that I become re-enchanted with everyday life. These glimpses I now share with you—a gentle stream of simple insights that flow through my life and, I hope, merge into yours.

I like to call them *Currents of the Heart*.

Currents of the Heart

PART ONE

Ripples
in the Stream

&

Not always talking to Him or about Him but
just waiting before Him...
Till the clouds lift...
Till the dust settles...
And the stream runs clear.

F.B. MEYER

Imaginations

⌘

*A*ram kissed us good-bye and walked out the front door.

"Pray for the Volkswagen!" he called over his shoulder.

I watched from the edge of the brick walk as he climbed into the little car and turned the key. The engine roared to life, but the Volkswagen shook and vibrated with such force and vigor I wondered how it could possibly make the long trip that lay ahead.

I waved until I could no longer see the shape of the funny fishing hat plopped on top of Aram's head. Bending down to pluck a dead leaf from a pink geranium, I said another quick prayer for the rusty, noisy little car and its precious cargo.

All day long I felt a sadness, an emptiness. I just don't like saying good-bye. I don't like having one of my children travel alone over many miles of busy freeways, passing through strange towns, sleeping in cheap motels, and eating who knows what—even if he is twenty years old.

By dinnertime we hadn't heard anything, so I had to assume all was well. My mother's heart, however, kept worrying.

All evening I eagerly answered the phone each time it rang, but no Aram. I got ready for bed and watched some pathetic late-night show on TV, trying to take my mind off the silent telephone on the table beside me. Finally I climbed into bed with a good book but found it impossible to concentrate. I lay there, my thoughts far away with Aram and his Volkswagen.

A verse from Isaiah kept playing over and over in my head—a verse I adapted for my own need. *You will keep her in perfect peace, whose mind is stayed on You.*

I glanced again at the clock. It was past midnight. Why hadn't he called? My mind conjured up all kinds of images. *He fell asleep at the wheel and went over an embankment. An eighteen-wheeler blew a tire and lost control, slamming into the little car. He's stranded somewhere on a dark freeway. He was mugged on his way to the motel room.*

Mothers have vivid imaginations—especially late at night when we're not sure where our children are.

It was then I remembered a marginal note on that "perfect peace" verse from Isaiah 26:3. It read, "Thou wilt keep him in perfect [superlative] peace whose imagination stops at Thee.... Because he trusteth in Thee."

We experience peace as we focus our thoughts and our vivid imaginations on the Father—and not on our concerns and worries.

"Lord," I prayed, "bring all of my thoughts into captivity.[1] Stop those worries with thoughts of You."

A small, quiet inner voice seemed to reply from the Psalms, "It is vain for you to sit up late. I give to My beloved sleep." (See Psalm 127:2.)

I slept.

Aram called the next morning. He was fine.

And so was I.

The Paper Heart

∽

*O*ur voices rose along with the intensity of the argument.
We exchanged words we didn't mean. We threw out
issues that weren't relevant. We rehashed past grievances,
forgiven but never forgotten.

Neither of us had intended our simple discussion to accelerate
into a heated argument.

It was late, and both of us were tired. Too tired. Stephan and I
had both endured a day-long parade of stress, tensions, and mini-
crises. I'd found myself pulled in ten different directions all day: the
children, laundry, groceries, writing deadlines, friends wanting
advice, letters needing answers, the jangling telephone. I felt fragmented and weary beyond description.

Stephan, too, had experienced an especially trying day, dealing
with men and women whose lives were falling apart. After an hour
of fighting traffic he arrived at home to find children clamoring for
his attention, a list of patients to call, and a stack of bills to be paid.
All evening we had been living on the edge of a scream, trying to
control our frayed nerves.

Then a minor disagreement accelerated way out of control.

As our words heated the air, the door to our bedroom cracked
open. Slowly. Quietly. A small hand reached through the opening

and placed something on the door. Then just as quietly the hand retreated and the door closed. Curious, I got up to investigate. Taped to the door I found a small paper heart colored with red crayon and emblazoned with the words "I love Mom and Dad."

Eight-year-old Antony was doing his part to try to make peace.

Suddenly I remembered the verse, "A little child shall lead them" (Isaiah 11:6 KJV). Shame-filled tears trickled down my face. Stephan and I looked at each other, both sorry for the way we had allowed our overtaxed emotions to control us and to upset our home.

There's no denying that life is full of stress and tension, and every family experiences times of conflict. The problem doesn't lie in the difficulties, tensions, or disagreements themselves, but in how we choose to *handle* them.

Most family conflicts can be resolved effectively if there is concern, communication, commitment...and large helpings of simple courtesy.

Today's tendency is to be so involved with our own problems that we really don't show heartfelt care for each other...and apathy is even worse than argument. We need to love each other unconditionally, unselfishly, and show our support in concrete ways. And then we need to communicate. Spend time together. Talk. Ask questions. And listen, listen, listen.

Do you know the secret desires and goals of your spouse? Do you know why your teenager is moody? Do you know why your nine year old is upset? Do you really listen to each other?

Communication, of course, takes time. Sometimes lots of it. It also takes commitment. Am I willing to sacrifice some of my own feelings and desires and interests for the good of the family? Am I willing to accept others just as they are, individuals with unique personalities, interests, and styles of expression? Can I handle the fact that we must sometimes simply agree to disagree?

Although a certain amount of conflict may be inevitable in every family, I've found a couple of secrets over the years that can help calm the troubled waters.

It has been said that more friction is caused by *tone of voice* than any other single factor. As much as I hate to admit it, I tend to be a screamer. And yet the Scriptures tell us, "A gentle answer turns away wrath, but a harsh word stirs up anger" (Proverbs 15:1). Yes, it may be necessary on occasion to confront one another or to express our feelings to family members...but next time, perhaps we could use a nicer tone of voice. It does work.

Timing is yet another key element. I'm the honest and straightforward type, and it's difficult for me to wait to express myself. But it's just plain unwise to throw a problem at my husband as soon as he steps through the front door...or for him to confront me just as I'm trying to get dinner on the table. The Bible praises "a word fitly spoken" (Proverbs 25:11 KJV) and remarks "how wonderful it is to be able to say the right thing at the right time!" (Proverbs 15:23 TLB).

Another peacekeeping tactic is simply *choosing to ignore* a harsh word or perceived slight. The best part of wisdom may be to let certain comments or remarks float right on by. The Bible instructs us to "turn the other cheek" (Matthew 5:39) and tells us that "love covers" (Proverbs 10:12) and that "love forgets mistakes" (Proverbs 17:9 TLB). In other words, some things just aren't worth a big blowup. Or even a little one. Perhaps before you allow yourself to respond or react, you might stop for a moment and ask yourself, "Five years from now, how important will this really be?"

I can't even remember what Stephan and I were arguing about when little Antony placed his paper heart on our bedroom door.

But we have left it there as a reminder.

"Bethlehem Was Never As Miserable As This!"

∽

*T*he holiday season had arrived again, brimming with joy and anticipation. But there was also the usual hustle and bustle of all the preparations—shopping, wrapping, decorating, and baking.

Finally everything was ready. We loaded into the car, and Stephan, the children, and I drove to my parents' home in North Carolina. That first glimpse of "home" always fuels our excitement and anticipation. It's almost as though we can smell the fresh apple pie and feel the warmth of a cozy fire before we get out of the car.

This excitement built to a crescendo on Christmas Eve as each child and adult hung his or her stocking from the fireplace mantle in the large living room. With a twinkle in his eye, Daddy gathered all of us around and placed a long distance call to Santa at the North Pole—just to make sure he'd received all the children's gift lists and to wish him a speedy trip.

As we tucked the children into bed, the unmistakable sound of sleigh bells jingled somewhere over the roof of the house. (My brother had hung donkey bells on the chimney.) Needless to say, sleep didn't come easily for the children that night!

When Christmas morning arrived, everyone rushed downstairs. A fire blazed merrily on the hearth, and the aroma of coffee and sweet rolls met us in the kitchen. By strict family tradition, no one is allowed into the living room where the Christmas tree stands guard over the bulging stockings and brightly wrapped gifts until *after* breakfast.

The children quickly inhaled a few bites and then sat waiting as patiently as possible. Finally the last drop of coffee was downed, and the eager faces of the children turned for the anticipated permission to rush into the living room.

But Daddy wanted to have devotions first. He announced that he would read the Christmas story. The children accepted this with a few audible sighs. Then, after the story and prayer, they jumped up out of their seats.

But once again they were disappointed. This time, my sister Anne suddenly said she wanted the children to line up and enter the living room one by one so she could take pictures.

That did it! My five-year-old son turned to his grandmother and said with utter exasperation and disgust, "Bethlehem was never as miserable as this!"

Later, smiling as I recalled my son's remark, I remembered another Christmas Eve. I recalled sitting on the floor with tears of exhaustion streaking down my cheeks as I wrapped gifts until long past midnight. My smile faded as I remembered just how miserable I'd felt that night. Something has happened to our holiday season that often makes it seem more of a burden than a blessing.

Have you ever wondered how that first Christmas Eve might

have been celebrated? Were the cherubim and the seraphim, angels of every description, hurriedly preparing to send the Lord of heaven down to earth in the form of a baby boy?

Perhaps on one side of heaven angels were working on the magnificent program they would present to the shepherds. Another angel might have been arranging to send that special star sailing across the skies to eventually guide the wise men to the little Messiah. Maybe another angel tenderly watched over Joseph and Mary as they made their way toward the stable.

Of course we don't know exactly what happened, but we do know that when all was ready, "God sent forth his Son" (Galatians 4:4 KJV). And all of heaven gathered as the King of kings and Lord of lords laid aside His glory, placing it at His Father's feet and saying, "A body hast thou prepared me.... Lo, I come...to do thy will, O God" (Hebrews 10:5, 7 KJV).

While the heavenly preparations might have been complex, the earthly men and women involved in the first Christmas kept it simple.

The hearts of a few willing people—Mary, Joseph, the shepherds, and the wise men—were simple. The site of the birth, a small stable in a small town, was simple. The celebration was simple: shepherds, hard-working men, left their work for a few hours to go and "see this thing which [had] come to pass" (Luke 2:15 KJV). And then they returned to their responsibilities.

The gifts were also simple, yet their value was priceless, timeless, and eternal:

—Joseph gave his obedience.

—Mary gave her body.

—The shepherds gave their adoration.

—The wise men gave their worship.

But then there were those who missed that first Christmas altogether:

—The innkeeper was too busy with the mundane cares of his guests.

—The guests themselves were too concerned with bodily comforts and personal affairs to be bothered with happenings in the stable.

—King Herod was too absorbed with his insecurities, his court, and his pathetic dreams of glory.

They were all too busy, too concerned, too wrapped up in other things.

I've been asking myself the past few years whether I have also missed Christmas. Have I been too busy, too preoccupied with material concerns and what others might think if things are not "just right"? Am I in danger of missing the real meaning of Christmas? I don't think for a moment the Lord would have us dampen the excitement of Christmas. After all, He Himself has given us "all things to enjoy" (1 Timothy 6:17 KJV).

Perhaps this year our Christmas lists should read:

more attention to our toddlers

more time and appreciation for our parents and our mates

more unconditional acceptance of our teenagers
more love and concern for our friends

And what about our gift to the One whose birthday we celebrate? All He asks is the gift of ourselves—with all our faults and failures, problems and fears. This is Christmas:

God giving,
our receiving,
God fulfilling.

Blessed Christmas!

Building Memories

∽

*T*he mountain air was cool and crisp, offering the perfect excuse to light the fire. Immediately the room was bathed in a soft glow, enveloping me in its warmth. It isn't often that I can slip away and spend a weekend here at my parents' mountain home without my children, and I was savoring this brief return to childhood.

The wood crackled cheerily, and Chester, the big gray cat, slept beside me. I snuggled down in the corner of the sofa, wrapping myself in happy memories.

This rambling home with its old log walls, its simple homey furniture, and its abundance of windows overlooking the Blue Ridge Mountains holds many memories for me. Memories of happy Christmas celebrations, fun birthdays, weddings, anniversaries, and delightful family times spent reading or sharing together. Memories of stimulating and sometimes heated conversations with various family members, guests, and friends. Memories of Daddy or Mother praying for each one of us by name. So much of what I know was learned in this mountain home.

In this home, Jesus became my best friend.

In this home, I learned to love the Scriptures.

In this home, I experienced for myself God's abiding love and faithfulness.

I got up and tossed another log onto the fire. Snuggling deeper into the soft cushions and pulling an afghan around my shoulders, I thought about how important and precious memories are—some good, some bad, some happy, some sad.

As I gazed into the soft, flickering flames, memories of a happy, contented childhood flooded my mind. ...*The tantalizing odors of homemade apple pie and southern fried chicken wafting from the kitchen...My grandfather on his knees praying early each morning...Playing in the woods with my brothers and sisters...Sibling squabbles that made us cry then, but make us laugh now...Hectic but happy mealtimes...Family devotions...Hiking the mountain ridges...Spending the night on my grandparents' sleeping porch...Picnics in my grandparents' backyard...Big family reunions.*

And yes, some not-so-happy memories, too.

Memories of taking Daddy to the train station and having to say good-bye again, sometimes knowing he wouldn't be back for six months. Memories of going away to boarding school at age twelve and the terrible homesickness I suffered. Memories of standing at the grave site of my precious grandparents.

However, as I thought back, I realized that most of my memories were happy. They almost *had* to be happy because of the atmosphere generated by the joyful, fun-loving Christians all around me. Warmed by my recollections as well as by the fire, my thoughts drifted next to my own children.

How thankful I am each time I hear them reminisce. They giggle and laugh as each one tries to outdo the others with happy stories of childhood. Often I find the children poring over the picture albums. They love to remember with each other and with us. And how grateful I am that most of their memories seem to be happy ones—in spite of all my mistakes.

As life becomes ever busier, more complex, and more hectic, I have to continually remind myself that *memories are still being made.* Each day I must be attentive to creating an atmosphere conducive to happy memories for the younger children. How important it is not only to pass on old memories but to create lasting, new ones...together. Warm, joyous memories. Fun, ridiculous, laughter-filled memories. Loving, sentimental memories.

As I write, rich in happy memories, I am aware that some of you reading this have not been privileged with such recollections. You may even cringe when you think of your childhood. Your only desire may be to forget.

I can only encourage you to take your hurtful memories to the foot of the cross and ask the Lord to cover them with His blood. Then allow Him to begin the precious healing process.

Your hurt may never go away completely. Some scars are very deep. Every now and then a memory may stab your heart with a searing pain. But through His love and with His help the pain can be lessened. He will gradually free you from the tyranny of your past and enable you to create a memory-building atmosphere in your home *now.*

Knowing that God has taken care of both our past and our future, we are free to make "now" all it can be.

Modeling

∽

*T*wo years had passed since we had seen my in-laws or Stephan's family. We were going to their home for dinner, proud and excited to show off our grandchildren, their great-grandchildren.

Our eldest grandson, Stetson, had just celebrated his fourth birthday; he didn't remember his great-grandfather, called "Papa." We arrived (all thirteen of us) at the appointed hour and were greeted at the front door. I watched the small children as they entered the home and were introduced to family members they did not know.

They quickly warmed to my beautiful, gentle, Swiss mother-in-law, who was celebrating her ninetieth birthday. But they were wary of Papa. Papa is Armenian, with heavy jowls, dark piercing eyes, and big bushy eyebrows. As we sat in the living room, waiting for dinner to be served, we enjoyed the antics of the small ones who were observing Papa from a distance as they played together on the carpet.

Soon we moved into the dining room, where a fragrant dinner awaited us. The long, formal table was set with the best china and silver. Glancing around the table at the soft candlelight illuminating each face, I breathed a silent thanks to God for the opportunity to be together.

Halfway through the meal, Papa looked at our eldest son,

Stephan-Nelson, sitting at the opposite end of the table trying to keep his three little ones quiet. In a burst of enthusiasm, Papa asked him to come and give him a kiss. With a smile, Stephan-Nelson got up, went to his grandfather, and gave him a hug.

Little Stetson, seeing his father hugging Papa, suddenly lost all fear. He ran across the room as fast as his legs could carry him and threw his tiny arms around his great-grandfather. Tears touched my eyes as I sat there realizing once again the importance of example.

I am continually amazed to see how our children imitate us—just as we model and imitate our own parents. I tremble when I think how often I fail to provide the model I want my children to imitate. Many times after falling short I ask the Lord to "please erase this memory from my children's minds." What an important and vital responsibility it is to set before our children a godly example to follow. I am so grateful for the examples I had growing up—examples of men and women living balanced, positive, fun-loving, yet disciplined Christian lives.

Someone once said that the best way to make a child eat his food is to see his parents thoroughly enjoying theirs. The Christians I grew up around made me hungry for what I saw them cherish. I longed to mirror their Christian character and lifestyles.

When I was a child, spending the night at my maternal grand-parents' house was always a treat. They lived just across the street, and many a night, already bathed and in my nightgown, I would grab my pillow and run over to their house. LaoNaing, the Chinese name I called my grandmother, always made me feel welcome and loved. She would usually give me a delicious baked custard sprinkled with cinnamon and nutmeg or a piece of cream pie before sending me upstairs to bed.

Early in the morning, I would crawl out of bed and creep down the stairs, knowing that Lao I, my grandfather, would be on his knees in front of the big, overstuffed rocking chair. I would stand there a moment or two watching him, feeling secure in the knowledge that he was also praying for me and wishing for me the same intimate relationship he shared with the Lord.

My grandmother was always doing for others. I can't remember a single day when she failed to call my mother and ask if there was anything she could do for her. What an unselfish, servant attitude she modeled!

I thought of how my own father sets before me an example of always looking at each situation he faces and each decision he makes from eternity's perspective.

Recently flying on a plane with my mother, Stephan observed that she is never idle; she's always reading, taking notes, jotting down ideas. He laughed and remarked that now he knew where I got my active mind.

But I also long to mirror her total reliance on the person of Jesus Christ, her love and knowledge of His Word, her keen sense of humor, and her acceptance of others just the way they are. My heart asks, *How can I set before my children these kinds of examples, the kinds I wish them to mirror and follow?*

Paul tells us in 1 Timothy, "Be their ideal; let them follow the way you teach and live; be a pattern for them in your love, your faith, and your clean thoughts" (4:12 TLB). This is the secret of example—living it honestly day by day to the best of our ability, with God's help.

And remember, we don't have to be perfect, but we do have to be *real*. Neither God nor our children expect us to be models of perfection. But we can become examples of men and women who genuinely love God and seek to follow Him with a whole and earnest heart.

Why Bother?

∽

The ominous storm clouds that formed over the Everglades had brought the usual summer-afternoon thunderstorm. But now the storm had rumbled on its way, and the hot sun was once again shining. Puffs of steam rose from the pavement.

Outside my window I noticed several red plastic cups lying around the yard along with the usual assortment of wet towels, bicycles, and toys of various shapes and sizes. Like the sun, the children had also reappeared. They emerged from various parts of the house like little bugs coming out after dark.

Summer survival had just begun. Once again, I faced the daunting dual challenges of keeping the children occupied and entertained while maintaining the house in some semblance of order.

One evening as I watched a popular TV show, I sympathized with a mother who stood in the kitchen surrounded by an after-breakfast chaos. As the children had inhaled their cereal and rushed to catch the school bus, they had left the table and counters in utter shambles. Dirty dishes were piled high beside the sink...which was clogged. (Her husband had forgotten his promise to fix it before he left for work.) As the harried mom surveyed the damage, she mused wryly, "No wonder some species eat their young."

I chuckled. But I know there's a dark side to the joke. There are days when we parents feel we cannot cope, when we wonder if it's worth all the effort and stress. Shortly after I had completed a book entitled *Thank You, Lord, for My Home,* I experienced one of those, "Is it worth it?" days while my mother happened to be visiting us.

The children were running around arguing over small, silly things when I suddenly realized the septic tank had overflowed. I quickly called the plumber. Just then the doorbell rang, and there stood the wallpaper man, ready to hang wallpaper. I helped him get set up, then hurried back into the fray to deal with the kids, get lunch started, and plan dinner. I was trying to get the laundry under control when the telephone rang and the plumber's truck arrived. With this, the dog began to bark, and the telephone rang—again. Through it all, Mother wrote down in her notebook all the activities going on that morning in the Tchividjian household.

Later, when I had a "free" moment, I found Mother in the family room, reviewing the several pages she had written. She looked up and said with a smile, "Honey, I think you should write a new book and entitle it *Lord, I Thanked You Too Soon for My Home.*"

Is a family worth all of the strain and stress? Has a home become more of a burden than a blessing? Why bother? For many, these questions may prompt disastrous steps. The home breaks up. Husbands want out from under the responsibility, wives seek significance by looking elsewhere for fulfillment, and children seek freedom and independence almost before they're old enough to speak.

When I experience a difficult day and sometimes ask myself these questions, I often allow my mind to drift back to the mountains of North Carolina. I consider anew the blessings I received from my family home there.

It provided for my physical, emotional, and material needs, but more than that, it provided for my spiritual needs. The framework of our home was our godly Christian heritage.

My home also provided security. I once asked one of my smaller children what he thought a home was, and he replied, "It's a place where you come in out of the rain." The home should be a warm sanctuary from the storms of life for each member of the family.

A home should provide love and acceptance. I always knew I would be loved and accepted in my home although my behavior was not always approved of. Husbands and wives need this kind of security as much as children do.

My home provided examples of love and commitment. I saw couples being "kind one to another, tenderhearted, forgiving one another" (Ephesians 4:32 KJV). That doesn't mean my parents didn't disagree at times. (Mother says "if two people agree on everything, one of them is unnecessary!")

My home also provided direction and discipline. I saw examples of Christians truly enjoying their faith.

Even if you weren't blessed with this sort of spiritual legacy during your growing up years, you can still *begin* such a heritage for your own children and grandchildren. How? By making sure of your personal relationship with the Lord Jesus and passing it on.

The home was the first institution ordained and blessed by God Himself. It was created for our good and for His glory. When God created the heavens and the earth, He said, "It is good." When He created the grass, the flowers, the fish, and the fowl, He said, "It is good." When He created the stars and the moon, He said, "It is good." When He created all the animals, He said, "It is good."

Then He created Adam, and He said, "It is *not good* that man should be alone." So God created Eve, thus forming the first home.

Proverbs says, "By wisdom a house is built" (24:3). The wisdom it takes to build a home can only come from God. We are told to ask Him for wisdom and He will give it to us.

In James we read, "The wisdom that comes from heaven is first of all pure and full of quiet gentleness. Then it is peace-loving and courteous.... It is full of mercy and good deeds. It is wholehearted and straightforward and sincere" (3:17 TLB).

What a beautiful picture of a Christian home. But it takes more than my husband or I have to achieve this kind of atmosphere. There are burdens as well as blessings in a home, and we don't always have the wisdom, strength, or patience to deal with them. But how wonderful that we can call on the One who does.

Why bother? Because the family is ordained and blessed by God. It is a blessing, not only to each member, but to our communities as well. We don't have to be perfect or have perfect families, but we have to be *real*... and allow the reality of the Lord to shine through.

Thoughts in a Grocery Aisle

∽

*M*y mouth began to water as I walked up and down the aisles of the grocery store in mid-November. I love turkey, stuffing, mashed potatoes, pecan pie, and all that makes Thanksgiving dinner so delicious.

But even in the midst of all that abundance, my thoughts kept returning to a place where people don't celebrate Thanksgiving.

A few months earlier my sister Anne and I had been privileged to participate in the first women's Bible conference ever held in Rumania. We drove into Rumania from Hungary, and as we crossed the border, we immediately noticed the difference. Rich, fertile fields grace the countryside of Hungary. Its towns are clean, and its shop windows are filled.

In contrast, Rumania, a country just beginning to experience a measure of freedom, is desperately poor. With the exception of its natural beauty and its warm, friendly people, its resources are few.

I looked at the gentle, stoic faces of the women gathered to study the Bible. Void of makeup and jewelry and dressed in dark, practical clothing, the women wore little color to brighten the room.

They had so little, and for most of them it had taken real effort and courage to attend this conference. Many had never before been away from home, never stayed in a hotel, never eaten in a restaurant.

Some had traveled for many hours in hot, crowded buses over bumpy roads to reach the conference site. Because Rumania is a male-dominated society, many of the women even had difficulty in getting their husband's permission to attend the conference.

The lives of these women are as difficult and as colorless as their surroundings. Most of them work long and hard in dingy offices or dreary factories only to return home to small, dilapidated apartments that often have to be shared with in-laws or other extended-family members.

With few modern conveniences, the simple tasks of shopping, cooking, and washing clothes are difficult and time consuming. The small, sparse shops display meager offerings on their shelves. A typical merchant has two or three unmatched glasses, a small tea set, a couple of blouses in odd sizes, a few simple toys, and no luxuries. These women have little in the way of material possessions, recreation, or even privacy to reward them for their hard work.

Sitting there watching their earnest faces soaking up every word, I thought, *Oh, how much I take for granted!* I thought of my comfortable house. The grocery stores filled with every kind of food. (Just try to count the varieties of cereal!) Discount and department stores piled high with everything and anything I need. Innumerable toy stores jammed with unnecessary playthings that break after one week. I thought of my closet full of brightly colored clothes, my air-conditioned car, my kitchen filled with conveniences that make life so easy.

And then I thought of how often I complain, how I mumble

about having to put away eight bags of groceries or unload the dishwasher. I fuss about all the laundry that needs washing (and God forbid that the washing machine or dryer ever break!). I grumble about driving the children to their various activities and gripe about cleaning the house.

I thought of the abundance of my life, the privileges I not only take for granted but have come to expect: freedom, churches, good books, Christian radio and TV programs, my home and family, health care, modern conveniences and comforts, even hot water, ice cubes, and clean sheets. Oh, how much I have, and how much I have to be thankful for!

In the last few years, Thanksgiving seems to have been swallowed up by the commercialization of Christmas. It's just squeezed in, and the meaning of Thanksgiving and the practice of setting aside a day to say "Thank You, Lord" seems all but lost.

The children are often more interested in making their Christmas lists than in giving thanks for what they already have. So I decided to try to emphasize Thanksgiving in a new way, to make a conscious effort to help my family be more aware of all we have to be thankful for. I noticed in Scripture that the writers often said, "Remember...." Remember how the Lord has cared for you; remember His faithful provisions of food and clothing....

So during the week of Thanksgiving, I remind my family every day to think of at least one thing the Lord has done for them personally.

During that week I play "I Spy God" with the family. I look for things in our everyday lives that come from God—and point them out to the children. For example, I spy God in providing Dad with a job. I spy God in keeping Aram safe while driving and in helping Jerushah adjust to her new school and in helping Antony catch that big fish. I spy God in protecting our home from the storm and in answering our prayers for sunshine for the party.

Then I remind them of how important it is not only to observe all that God has done for us, but also to express our thanks with a special prayer of thanksgiving. It is so easy to take our many blessings for granted. But during that week, I encourage my family not to ask for anything but instead to concentrate on saying "Thank You, Lord" for all that we have.

It's a lesson I learned from some long-suffering women in Rumania. When you have next to nothing, you take nothing for granted. When you receive what you've never been privileged to receive before, your thanksgiving knows no bounds.

God help me to remember.

A Blessing from the Birds

⚘

Said the robin to the sparrow,
"I should really like to know
Why these anxious human beings
Rush around and worry so."

Said the sparrow to the robin,
"Friend, I think that it must be
That they have no heavenly Father
Such as cares for you and me."[1]

ELISABETH CHENEY

After days of steady rain there were now patches of blue in the overcast sky outside my kitchen window. The sun was even beginning to peek out timidly between the clouds.

The chimes on the grandfather clock reminded me that the children would soon be bounding in from school, tired and hungry. It was almost time to start fixing their dinner, but maybe I could take just a few minutes....

When I slid open the glass door, a surge of warm, humid air greeted me. I was concerned about a number of things and felt the need to take advantage of this quiet moment, knowing it wouldn't last for long.

I sat down in one of the old rocking chairs on the porch.

Glancing appreciatively around the yard, I noticed that everything seemed to be celebrating the return of the sun. The grass was a bright and vivid shade of green; the bougainvillea bush was once again loaded with blossoms. Masses of fuchsia, white and orange, intertwined and tumbled down both sides of the fence. *It looks almost gaudy*, I thought as I watched a very brave (or very stupid) gray squirrel sneak up and steal a piece of dog food right from under the nose of Jessie, our good-natured but overweight rottweiler.

Then a bold blue jay suddenly swooped down, grabbed what morsel he could from Jessie's bowl, and quickly flew off again before Jessie—or even the squirrel—had time to notice.

A pair of gentle mourning doves tiptoed timidly around the edge of the porch, and on the top of the olive trees, a mockingbird sang its heart out.

A family of very fat black-and-white ducks with red heads loitered off to the left in the shade of a ficus tree, the staging area for their daily excursion across the backyard. One of them, apparently the appointed lookout, slowly edged closer. When he felt it was safe, he signaled the others. Quickly, they queued up into a long line and waddled across the terrace as fast as their webbed feet would go. They too stopped at Jessie's dish, hoping to find leftovers.

I laughed as I watched their obvious disappointment upon discovering an empty bowl (the blue jay and squirrel had beaten them to it that day). They slowly retreated and waited patiently in the grass, sending their scout from time to time to see if Jessie's dish had been replenished.

While sitting there, rocking gently back and forth, contemplating my concerns and observing this mixture of wildlife scurrying and flitting about the yard, I remembered the passage in Matthew 6 that tells us not to worry.

How I needed to be reminded of that—especially at that moment! I find myself becoming overly concerned, anxious about unpaid bills…my parents' health…a wayward child…my husband's job situation…the lump discovered in my friend's breast…the children's safety…my writing deadlines…my elderly mother-in-law's pending surgery…all of my various responsibilities and my own lack of physical and emotional strength.

My thoughts were suddenly distracted by the loud, rhythmic tapping of a ladder-backed woodpecker working his way up the side of a palm tree while a regal, great blue heron walked stealthily along the edge of the lake. Then a flash of bright orange caught my attention. On the fence, contrasted against the brilliant pink backdrop of the bougainvillea blossoms, two orioles waited to attack the berries on a neighboring bush.

I thought again of that passage in Matthew: "Look at the birds! They don't worry about what to eat—they don't need to sow or reap or store up food—for your heavenly Father feeds them. And you are far more valuable to him than they are. Will all your worries add a single moment to your life?" (6:26–27 TLB).

Not long ago, while preaching from this passage, our pastor asked if we ever wondered why the Lord had chosen to use birds in this particular lesson. Personally, I had never thought about it. But Pastor Mike suggested that maybe it was because birds, who are small creatures, limited in size and strength, are capable of doing only so much at a time. Birds can carry only one twig at a time while building their nests, carry only one worm at a time to feed their babies, take care of only the most important, most urgent task at a time. This keeps them focused. Their priorities are in the right order because they can do no differently.

I, on the other hand, become overly concerned and anxious because I overload every area of my life. I overdo and overindulge my schedule...my budget...my nerves...my strength...my expectations. I seem to stay in a perpetual state of anxiety, whereas birds do only what they can, day by day, little by little, in complete and total dependence upon their loving heavenly Father.

No wonder the birds sing their little hearts out!

They sing because they're happy

They sing because they're free.

For His eye is on the sparrow

And I know He watches me.[2]

Suddenly Jessie began to bark, alerting me that a car had just come up the drive. The children were home.

With a much lighter and very grateful heart, I pulled myself out of my reverie and my rocker and went to greet them while the ducks, ever hopeful, began to waddle once again toward the dog's dish.

> Be anxious for nothing, but in everything by prayer and
> supplication, with thanksgiving, let your requests be made
> known to God (Philippians 4:6 NKJV).

Where Are the Front Lines?

❦

I want to be on the front lines," I complained to my friend. "You know, on the mission field somewhere in the deepest jungle— or high up in a remote village clinging to the side of a mountain in the Himalayas."

"I know what you mean," she sighed. "Carpooling, folding laundry, and washing dishes just isn't my idea of being on the cutting edge of service."

"Exactly," I said. "The problem with my life is that it's so…mundane, so…daily."

"Well," my friend continued, "maybe when our children are grown, we could go to Africa and help with the orphans—or to Eastern Europe and encourage the believers there. Or maybe we could work in some war zone like Croatia or Bosnia."

I laughed. "My problem is, by the time all my children are grown, I'll be too *old*."

The Lord must have smiled at that, too. But He knew my desires, and not long after that conversation He led me to a little devotional that encouraged my heart. It was a piece written by a little French maid servant way back in the seventeenth century— when daily duties were much more difficult.

She wrote:

As soon as I woke in the morning I threw myself in the arms of Divine Love as a child does into its father's arms. I rose to serve Him and to perform my daily labor simply that I might please Him. If I had time for prayer, I fell on my knees in His divine presence, consecrated myself to Him, and begged Him that He would accomplish His holy will perfectly in me and through me, and that He would not permit me to offend Him in the least thing all through the day.

I occupied myself with Him and His praise as long as my duties permitted. Very often, I had not leisure to say even so much as the Lord's Prayer during the day; but that did not trouble me. I thought it as much my duty to work for Him as to pray to Him, for He Himself had taught me that all that I should do for love of Him would be a true prayer.

I loved Him and rejoiced in Him. If my occupations required all of my attention, I had nevertheless my heart towards Him; and as soon as they were finished, I ran to Him again, as to my dearest Friend. When evening came and everyone went to rest, I found mine in the Divine Love, and fell asleep still loving and adoring Him.[1]

Lives and responsibilities that seem a bit mundane, ordinary, commonplace…when lived and performed for Him become a sweet-smelling sacrifice, and that is extraordinary.[2]

In reality, each of us is on the front lines of service. In His providence He has placed us just where He wants us to be: in the roles of mothers, fathers, students, accountants, lawyers, pastors, secretaries, yes, even maids...for His glory.

A Vision of Forgiveness

∽

*H*ave you ever felt the need for forgiveness…or perhaps the need to forgive?

I meet so many people who are paralyzed in their present circumstances because they're chained to something in their past. They are either unable to forgive or to accept the fact that they are truly forgiven.

I once heard of a priest in a small midwestern parish who as a young man had committed what he felt was a terrible sin. Although he had asked God's forgiveness, all his life he carried around the burden of this sin. He just could not be sure God had really forgiven him.

One day he was told of an elderly woman in his congregation who sometimes had visions. During these visions, he had heard, she would often have conversations with the Lord. After a while the priest finally got up enough courage to visit this woman.

She invited him in and offered him a cup of tea. Toward the end of his visit, he set his cup down on the table and looked into the old woman's eyes.

"Is it true that sometimes you have visions?" he asked her.

"Yes," she replied.

"Is it also true that—during these visions—you often speak with the Lord?"

"Yes," she said again.

"Well...the next time you have a vision and speak with the Lord, would you ask Him a question for me?"

The woman looked at the priest a little curiously. She had never been asked this before. "Yes, I would be happy to," she answered. "What do you want me to ask Him?"

"Well," the priest began, "would you please ask Him what sin it was that your priest committed as a young man?"

The woman, quite curious now, readily agreed.

A few weeks passed, and the priest again went to visit this woman. After another cup of tea he cautiously, timidly asked, "Have you had any visions lately?"

"Why yes, I have," replied the woman.

"Did you speak with the Lord?"

"Yes."

"Did you ask Him what sin I committed as a young man?"

"Yes," the woman replied, "I did."

The priest, nervous and afraid, hesitated a moment and then asked, "Well, what did the Lord say?"

The woman looked up into the face of her priest and replied gently, "The Lord told me He could not remember."

"You see, if we confess our sins, He is faithful and just to forgive us our sins, our shortcomings, our failures, and to cleanse us from all of them...from everything" (1 John 1:9).

God not only forgives our sins, He also chooses to *forget* them. The Bible tells us He takes them and buries them in the deepest sea.

And then, as Corrie ten Boom used to say, "He puts up a sign that says 'No Fishing Allowed.'"

I can almost hear the priest as he walked briskly along the path back to his church, singing...

"Oh, the wonderful grace of Jesus,
Greater than all my sin;
How shall my tongue describe it,
Where shall its praise begin?
Taking away my burden,
Setting my spirit free;
For the wonderful grace of Jesus reaches me.

Wonderful, the matchless grace of Jesus
Deeper than the mighty rolling sea;
Wonderful grace, all-sufficient for even me.
Broader than the scope of my transgressions,
Greater far than all my sin and shame.
O magnify the precious name of Jesus,
Praise His name!"[1]

The Concert

I had looked forward all day to the concert that evening. I insisted on leaving early so we could get good seats, worried that the hall would be filled since the previous year's concert had been such a hit. After I had fussed and told everyone to "Hurry up!" we all piled into the various cars and took off.

We arrived in plenty of time—so early, in fact, that the doors weren't even open. (Of course the kids and Stephan gave me a hard time about this.) But as soon as it was permitted, we rushed in and grabbed good seats in the middle of the hall. A half hour later the concert began.

It wasn't long before I realized this concert was very different from what I had expected and anticipated. I endured it until the end...but just barely.

Later, as we were leaving, I felt disappointed and empty, and wondered why. After all, it had been a Christian concert. Was it just the overwhelming volume that had bothered me? It had been very loud.

No, that wasn't it. I had attended other, even louder concerts with the kids, and although the music hadn't pleased my middle-aged ears, I'd never left the concert hall feeling as empty as I was feeling right then.

Maybe it just wasn't my style. Maybe it was out of sync with my personal taste. After all, I much prefer Bach or Mozart or even Jimmy Buffet and Neil Diamond.

But no, that wasn't it either. I'm an open-minded person and try not to be judgmental or force my personal likes and dislikes on others. After all, as Mother has often said, "you don't have to like worms to go fishing!"

So what was it?

This particular concert seemed to have been just a bunch of noise. Nothing more. I didn't see how this cacophony of musical worms could have caught even one fish. It disturbed me until I fell asleep, and it was still bothering me when I awoke the next morning.

I poured a cup of coffee, and as I read my devotions and prayed, the Lord seemed to be telling me not to become overly concerned about it but just to file it in the "make a joyful noise" category and let it go at that.

But I was still troubled. *Why did it affect me so negatively?*

I turned the pages of my Bible and read about the big concert Solomon held to celebrate the completion of the temple. It must have been loud, for there were not only singers, cymbals, harps, and psalteries (stringed instruments) but 120 trumpets as well!

The writer of this account tells us, "The trumpeters and singers joined in unison, as with one voice, to give praise and thanks to the LORD. Accompanied by trumpets, cymbals and other instruments, they raised their voices in praise to the LORD.... Then...the glory of the LORD filled the temple of God" (2 Chronicles 5:13–14).

"That's it!" I cried. "That's the difference!"

The significance of the music is not the volume or the crowd or the kind of instruments or even the type of music. It's His glory. His glory has to be present.

In this particular concert, one person had taken center stage and drawn all of the audience's attention, manipulating and working the fans into a frenzy. Instead of lifting up the person of Jesus, this musician had just repeated and screamed the name of Jesus louder and louder while jumping higher and higher and dancing harder and harder. I'd gone away empty because contrived music/noise and not the presence of the Spirit of God had filled the place.

With my uneasiness finally resolved, I walked into the kitchen to refill my coffee cup. As I did, my eyes fell on a large sheet of white notebook paper prominently placed.

Mom, please call Ticketmaster today and get tickets for the concert. The sooner you call, the better the seats. I love you.

Antony

"Oh no," I groaned, "not *again*."

Yes, perhaps I should have been thankful that my twelve year old was so excited about going to another Christian concert. But since the last one had left my ears ringing, my head pounding, and my soul totally empty, I wasn't exactly relishing another such experience.

Antony's eagerness, however, won the day. I went out in the rain to get the tickets.

The day of the concert arrived and, once again, the place was jammed with young people. There were thousands of them, all screaming, yelling, dancing, jumping, and doing "the wave." Paper airplanes floated down from the upper levels like confetti, and I found myself thinking, *Gigi, what are you doing here?*

Then the young group arrived on stage to thunderous applause and the stomping of thousands of teenage feet. I got a little concerned when I saw a couple of older, more seasoned saints inconspicuously slip earplugs into their ears.

The concert began. Yes, it was loud...VERY LOUD! But there was a difference. These performers were here to entertain, yes; to perform professionally, yes; but also to lift up the person of Jesus Christ. Here it was evident that there was a "sweet, sweet Spirit in this place."[1] A LOUD one, but a sweet one.

Antony had a great time...and so did I.

Into the Wind

∽

I pulled my Chevy Blazer into the schoolyard, checking once again to make sure I hadn't forgotten the picnic or the kite. I smiled, remembering Antony's delight when I had agreed to drive for his class field trip on "kite day."

Upon entering his classroom, I found twenty children bursting with excitement. Grabbing their kites and bag lunches, they ran down the stairs and piled into the various cars and vans, and we were on our way.

When we arrived at the designated park, we mothers did our best to help these enthusiastic first-graders assemble their assorted kites. Then we spent the rest of the day assisting and encouraging small, frustrated fliers. We untangled kite string, did our utmost to get kites up and airborne, disengaged kites from trees, tried to comfort those whose kites broke, and pulled kites in when they got too high. As I watched all the brightly colored pieces of plastic soaring high above me, I thought, *Oh how I wish my children would soar through life as easily and gracefully as these kites!*

Just then, one of the kites came crashing to the ground, and a mother quickly rushed to the aid of the teary-eyed owner. The kite had developed a small tear, but the mother patiently mended the offending hole and helped the child get his kite airborne again. I looked around at the other children's kites. Some were struggling to get up, but quite a few were falling into trees and becoming entangled in the branches.

Children are not so different from these kites, I decided. They come in various shapes, sizes, and colors. They need someone to help them get started. Some children take a long time to discover the wind, and they struggle again and again to get up. Others seem to catch on quickly and sail through life with ease.

As I sat on the grass contemplating the kites, Antony suddenly came running up to me. "Mama," he cried, tears filling his big blue eyes, "my kite fell and the stick broke." I did my best to help him mend his broken kite, but I couldn't repair the damage. I put my arm around him and gave him a hug, trying to console him. My heart ached for this little fellow, and I longed to be able to fix his kite.

How often we parents wish we could fix the hurts and disappointments our children experience. How we long to protect them from the entanglements and defeats they encounter, but too often we can't. We hope our sons will soar and our daughters will fly through life with ease and grace. But most of them will get tangled up now and then and need someone to help repair the mess they've made. Some will suffer an emotional tear or two, and others will experience a break in family relationships, a divorce, or a broken heart. All children will fall from time to time. They will all suffer disappointments and failures, and when they do, they will need loving, patient, tender repair and encouragement before they're able to soar once again.

Like kites, children were created to fly. But they need wind—the undergirding and strength that comes from their parents' uncondi-tional love, acceptance, encouragement, and prayer. I thought of what David said of his son, "Prayer...shall be made for him contin-ually; and daily shall he be praised" (Psalm 72:15 KJV). Prayer and praise...these are the wind beneath a child's wings.

But sometimes as a parent I too lose the power to stay up, and sometimes I tumble and suffer disappointment and defeat. The Scriptures remind us that the wind beneath *our* wings is the faith we have in the unseen yet unfailing power of the Holy Spirit of God. I have discovered that the only way I can take courage and persevere is to depend wholly on His strength.

Isaiah shared this secret: "They that wait upon the LORD shall renew their strength; they shall mount up with wings as eagles" (40:31 KJV). God is our source of courage and determination, and because of Him we will persevere to the end. We will "run, and not be weary; and...walk, and not faint" (40:31 KJV).

I looked again at the brightly colored kites flying high above me in the blue sky. "Lord," I prayed, "give me Your wisdom to help my children catch the wind of Your Holy Spirit and to wait upon You so they will be able to mount up with eagles' wings, to run and not be weary, and to walk steadily through life without fainting."

PART TWO

Rapids and Whirlpools

∽

Have patience....
All things are difficult
Before they become easy.

SOURCE UNKNOWN

God's 9·1·1 Line

∽

*I*t doesn't take much to make me cross. I tend to have a low frustration level, especially in the morning before I've had a cup of coffee.

I remember one morning some years ago when, before I'd had that first important cup, quite a number of small, insignificant problems converged upon me all at once.

I'd been up several times during the night with a new baby, so when the alarm went off, I groaned in disbelief. Slowly I pulled myself out of bed and groped my way downstairs toward the coffeepot.

I hadn't even reached the stairs before I heard voices—loud voices—coming from the kitchen. Timidly opening the door I discovered a before-school free-for-all taking place. Gathering what little strength I had, I tried to ignore it just long enough to reach the coffeepot.

As I crossed the kitchen, the two year old spilled a glass of orange juice. I couldn't believe how far one little glass of juice could go. *Everywhere!*

Detouring to the broom closet, I grabbed the mop. Just as I finished cleaning up the spilled juice, the five year old spilled his. Before the second cleanup was complete, it was time for the four older children to leave for school.

Suddenly, Stephan-Nelson, the oldest, remembered that he had neither done his chores nor gathered his scattered gym clothes. The five year old screamed—for no apparent reason—then hit the two year old, who began to wail. I grabbed for the five year old (still no coffee) and yelled at the oldest—who seemed frozen in place—to get *moving*. The nine year old decided this was a good time to keep things stirred up by ridiculing his older brother. When I scolded him, he had the nerve to answer back and argue with me.

Still no coffee…

As if this were not enough, Stephan-Nelson turned to me and said, "If having seven kids is like this, I don't want *any*. And why did you have so many anyway?"

Hurt, I somehow managed to comb the different heads of hair, wash the remains of breakfast off their faces, help do the chores, and hustle the older children out the door. Then I wearily turned again toward the coffeepot—and caught the two year old drinking the bottle of pancake syrup. He saw the look in my eye, and before I could reach him, he hurriedly turned the bottle upside down and poured syrup all over the carpet. I felt myself slipping into a long, loud scream.

And I still hadn't had any coffee.

Sometimes, as on that chaotic morning, I'm at my wit's end, spending all my energy on foolish arguments, needless messes, senseless "emergencies," confusion, and noise till I have nothing left to give.

I discovered early in life that in times like these what I need is simply to be alone with the Lord. Coming quietly and reverently into His presence changes my attitude and my disposition. I follow the advice of Isaiah: "Enter your chambers, and shut your doors behind you; hide yourself, as it were, for a little moment, until the indignation is past" (26:20 NKJV). Usually if I can slip off alone with the Lord, it doesn't take long for me to settle down and feel rejuvenated enough to tackle whatever comes next.

But some days are so hectic I simply don't have time to slip away. Recently I had one of those days. The kids, the grandchildren, the weather, the telephone, the leak in the roof, the broken garbage disposal, my hormones—everything was out of control. And we were expecting *fifty* guests for lunch!

At such times instant, spontaneous prayers are called for, the "Oh, Lord, please help me!" kind of prayers.

At those moments I understand how Peter must have felt when he looked around at his situation—deep water, choppy seas, wind and waves all around—and suddenly remembered he could not really walk on water after all. Realizing he was vulnerable and feeling circumstances out of control, Peter panicked and began to sink. But on his way down, he called out, and immediately the Lord reached out His hand and lifted him up.

Just as the Lord pulled a sinking Peter out of the Sea of Galilee, so He has rescued me time and again when I was about to be swallowed up by my circumstances. The winds and waves of life batter and buffet me—tensions, pressures, finances, illness, fatigue, misunderstandings, unwelcome news, or just the busyness of everyday responsibilities. I feel so overwhelmed—and I take my eyes off the Lord and begin to sink under the load. But on my way down, I call out, "Lord, save me!" And He reaches out His hand....

The apostle Paul, however, reminds me not to wait until I'm sinking. He says, "Pray continually" (1 Thessalonians 5:17) or, in the King James Version, "Pray without ceasing." This means I am to keep the lines of communication with God open at all times.

I was so touched and encouraged by something F. B. Meyer once wrote: "Of course there will be times when we shall deliberately bow our knees unto the Father; but there will be many more when we shall have access to Him in a swift-winged thought, a tear hastily brushed away, a yearning, an ejaculation, a loving, restful glance of mutual understanding. Strange that we make so little of these wonderful opportunities of access to the Father."[1]

Yes, it helps to slip away to a quiet place whenever you can. Get on your knees with a prayer journal whenever you can. Enjoy an extended conversation with your heavenly Father whenever you can.

And remember, God does not have call waiting or voice mail, but He does have a 9-1-1 line. And He answers every call.

Even before you've had your coffee.

P.S. Stephan-Nelson, the one who vowed he would "never have children," is now married with several children of his own.

When We Are Afraid

∽

*T*he day was unbearably hot. Over ninety-five degrees in the shade, and nothing seemed to offer relief from the obsessive heat.

Then, late in the afternoon, it began to grow dark. I looked outside and saw that the whole western sky was black. Thick, dark clouds soon billowed over our house. The thunder began, soft rolls at first, almost like the sounds of a bowling game, then louder and louder, like waves crashing upon a rocky shore.

Lightning flashed, the lights flickered, and with a pop the TV—which was helping to keep nine-year-old Antony's mind off the frightening storm—suddenly went blank.

Antony was petrified. I tried to calm his fears, telling him how cozy it was inside our comfortable house and reminding him we had candles, food, and each other. But to no avail.

Crash! The thunder clapped again right over the house. Jagged streaks of lightning lit up the black sky. Antony shrieked. (It didn't help that just the year before a close friend had been struck by lightning while horseback riding, killing the horse and almost killing our friend.)

"Antony, it's really OK," I soothed. "We're safe inside the house."

The storm continued for most of the evening, but fortunately it quieted somewhat by the time Antony had to go to bed. I was pleased to see that he was calmer and didn't seem to have a problem going to sleep.

The next morning I came into Antony's room and cheerily called, "Time to get up!" Bright sunshine flooded the room as I opened the shutters. The storm was over.

Then I noticed the tennis shoes.

Antony's sneakers—all of them—formed a line on the windowsill.

"What's this?" I asked him. "What are all these doing here?"

As he stretched and rubbed his sleepy eyes, he answered proudly, "Oh, I put them there so the rubber soles would protect me from the lightning."

I burst out laughing. Bless him, no wonder he fell asleep without a problem!

We all experience fears. Although I don't think of myself as a fearful person, a strange noise at night when Stephan is away and I am alone with the children causes my heart to race faster. We live in a dangerous world, and for most of us fear is a reality.

Children especially seem to go through phases when they are fearful. In addition to lightning, Antony, for some reason, is afraid of helicopters. When one flies over our house, he comes running inside. The fear is totally unwarranted—but very real to him!

Being a Floridian, Antony also feels cautious about hiking or exploring in the woods by himself around my parents' house in North Carolina. His cousins, who were raised in those woods, laugh at him, but Antony knows that bears prowl those areas now and then and that snakes live under the rocks and slither over the paths. And no one has to remind him of the mountain lion we spotted last year. He's afraid of those things.

I have friends who have a major panic attack if they see a cockroach. Others stand on tables to avoid a little mouse. Those sort of creepy-crawly things don't bother me much.

What I fear is making a fool of myself or of causing disappointment.

Most of all, I fear failure.

How can we face our fears and help each other deal with them?

I love to fly. I especially enjoy the feel of the powerful engines on takeoff. But once airborne, if the plane suddenly hits an air pocket or if we encounter a storm and turbulence, I get a little nervous. I like to fly, but I don't like rough flights.

When I'm on a bumpy flight, the first thing I do (after grabbing the arms of my seat) is to watch the reaction of the flight attendants. If they continue serving or walking around and talking normally to passengers and each other, I remain totally calm. If they take their seats but show no anxiety, I'm still calm. But every now and then, the flight attendants sense something more serious. They glance at each other with that special "this is more serious" kind of look and quickly take their seats.

At that point, I'm one nervous lady.

I find this same dynamic at work with my children. If Stephan and I show fear, they too are fearful. But when we remain calm and they sense that everything is under control, they feel secure.

Mother was raised in China at a period in history when warlords and bandits controlled the country. She doesn't remember a night during her childhood when she didn't fall asleep hearing gunfire. But when asked if she was ever afraid, she says, "No, because LaoNaing and Lao I [her parents] never showed the slightest fear."

If those we associate with tend to be fearful, their fear will probably rub off on us too. If others around us panic, we probably will too. Fear is contagious.

We need to learn to face our fears. I don't know why Antony is afraid of helicopters, but I know it helps alleviate his fears if I show him a magazine article about helicopters. Together, we read how they're used in difficult rescue operations or what is involved in learning to pilot one. Sometimes we'll watch a TV program about helicopters. The more familiar we are with the object of our fear, the less fear we experience.

But most of all, to combat our fears, we need to believe in and trust our loving God. From their first days I have done all I can to instill in my children and grandchildren the reality of a powerful, loving God who deeply cares for them. The Scriptures certainly seem to imply that each child of God has an angel in heaven who has direct access to the heavenly Father (Matthew 18:10).

One of the very first Bible verses I was taught was from the Psalms of King David: "The angel of the LORD encamps all around those who fear Him, And delivers them" (34:7 NKJV). The Scriptures are full of verses to comfort us in our fears: "Have...wisdom...and common sense.... With them on guard you can sleep without fear...for the Lord is with you; he protects you" (Proverbs 3:21, 24–26 TLB), and "When I am afraid, I will put my confidence in you. Yes, I will trust the promises of God" (Psalm 56:3–4 TLB).

Fear is demolished in direct proportion to our trust in God.

The Dangers of a Call-Waiting Lifestyle

∽

*W*onderful! I thought as I finished my coffee, *I have the whole day free. Now I'll reap the rewards of the long hours I put in yesterday so I'd have time to write today.*

I quickly threw a load of wash in the machine, emptied the dishwasher, fed the cat, checked on the dogs, and straightened the house, aiming to be at my desk by nine o'clock.

Just as I finished picking up the last room, the telephone rang.

"Mom…" I immediately recognized the voice of my teenage son. "I forgot my paper. Could you please bring it to the school? It's important."

Trying hard to sound pleasant, I replied, "Sure, honey." But inwardly I sighed, frustrated by this disturbance. I got dressed, climbed into the car, and drove to the school. *This is so typical of my days,* I thought as I walked to the student affairs office. *I work and plan carefully only to experience one interruption after another.*

Often my plans are interrupted by simple, mundane things like a son who forgets his homework or by the little phrase, "Mom, I don't feel well," which causes me to rearrange my whole day because of an unexpected fever. Frequently the phone rings just as I'm running out the door to keep an appointment. *Should I ignore it?* I ask myself. But being a mother, I think it might be one of the children needing me. So I run back and pick up the receiver only to hear a computerized voice selling magazines, insurance, or cemetery plots—or perhaps the dentist's office reminding me I'm past due for a checkup. This delay is just enough to cause me to have to rush, praying for green lights and fussing inwardly at the slow driver who won't move over. I arrive at my appointment out of breath, nerves frayed. Some days are so hectic I feel as if my life is just one big "call waiting"—one interruption interrupting another interruption.

One day I began to think about all the interruptions in my life, and I asked myself, *Could there be hidden blessings in these interruptions?*

I thought of how often Jesus was interrupted, how many times He was distracted and disturbed or delayed by those in need along His path. Remember the time Jesus was on His way to heal Jairus's daughter? This desperate father was anxious to get home with Jesus because his little girl was near the point of death. But as they made their way to the man's house, a despondent woman reached out and touched Jesus. Jesus stopped, looked around, and asked who had touched Him. When the woman finally came forward, Jesus spent precious moments reassuring and encouraging her.

Just then some men came from the ruler's house saying, "Don't bother Jesus any more, Jairus. It's too late. Your little girl is dead."

I wonder what rush of emotions the ruler experienced, what questions he must have asked, what resentment he must have felt for the poor woman who had interrupted and delayed them…just long enough to allow his precious little girl to die.

But even this interruption held a hidden blessing. The woman was not only encouraged, but she was also healed of her illness. Then Jesus continued on with a very distressed Jairus and performed an even greater miracle. He took the dead girl by the hand and brought her back to life (Mark 5:22–42).

As I looked at Scripture, I began to discover that yes, there are often hidden blessings in interruptions, delights in distractions, and rewards and satisfactions in delays. In each instance when Jesus was interrupted or delayed, He responded not with impatience and frustration but with patience and tenderness.

Recently when I was working against the clock to meet a deadline, the phone rang, and I heard the desperate voice of a friend. "Gigi, do you have a minute?"

I thought about my deadline, then I thought about Jesus and His reactions to interruptions. How would He have responded?

"Of course," I answered gently.

After a few moments I realized this friend needed me. I turned off the computer, got in my car, and took her to lunch. At the end of the day, my deadline still faced me, but I experienced the reward of a deep, inner satisfaction.

Not only are there hidden blessings in the interruptions that disturb us each day, but there are also lessons in values and priorities. I have discovered that often what I consider important may not be what is truly important from God's perspective.

From His point of view, spending time with my sick child who caused me to cancel my plans may be of more value than the appointment I'd scheduled. Perhaps taking the forgotten paper to school taught my teenager more about love and servanthood than a Sunday sermon. I know that encouraging my friend was of more value to both of us than comfortably meeting my deadline.

So I am trying to learn to concentrate less on the frustrating aspects of my call-waiting lifestyle and to focus my attention on the hidden blessings that can be found in a life filled with distractions and detours.

Jesus met interruptions with grace, compassion, and healing power. He can teach this sometimes-frazzled daughter of His how to do the same thing.

Frazzled

∽

*T*ired from putting away fifteen bags of groceries, I sat in the big wicker rocker, leafing through the magazine I'd picked up at the checkout counter. As I flipped through the pages, a word suddenly popped off one of the pages, bright as a neon sign.

"Frazzled!"

That's it! I said to myself. *That describes just the way I feel!*

I don't know if it was because I was facing a manuscript dead-line...or that I was in the throes of summer with the kids home all day...or because we were trying to sell our home of fifteen years...or because of the numerous out-of-town trips I'd had to take recently... or simply because of middle age.

Whatever the reason, I felt frazzled—and frustrated and fragmented too!

Our home stays in constant motion. A friend of mine recently tried to describe being under the Tchividjian roof to another friend. He said, "I just love being at Gigi's house. It's just so...so...so totally out of control!"

It *is* a lively home, to say the least. There are countless interruptions to deal with, arguments to mediate, children to chauffeur, people to encourage, neighbors to talk with, dogs to walk, wildlife to observe, grandchildren running in and out, telephones to answer, and (of course) call waiting to interrupt my interruptions. No wonder I sometimes feel a bit frazzled!

I keep telling myself I should be able to organize better, choose more wisely, handle children and deadlines with more patience, and show the house to prospective buyers, all in a more *serene* way.

"Gigi," I tell myself, "you don't need to live in this state of semi-panic. You don't need to wake up feeling so wired each morning."

My husband, Stephan, a wise man and an experienced counselor, has tried to teach me that life is full of trade-offs and choices. He has taught me that I really do have some control over the events in my life and that I can make choices to help me better manage the tensions and stresses.

For example...

Choosing my battles. Which battles are really worth fighting? Is it worth all the emotional effort to make the kids eat their peas? With my first child I decided it was. I would put the peas in his mouth, then hold his mouth shut until he swallowed them. Six children later, I've decided it is *not* worth the battle.

Am I wiser...or just running out of steam? I'm not sure.

Facing reality. Life has changed, and we can't fight it. In most homes today, both parents have to work. There are simply not enough hours in the day to do all we may wish to do. We may have to buy cookies rather than make them from scratch. We can't go back to the "good old days," and maybe, if we were honest, we really wouldn't want to go back.

Learning to say no. I may sometimes have to say no to good things in order to say yes to better things. Recently I had to make a very difficult decision and say no to a tempting and interesting opportunity because I was afraid it would cause too much stress and tension in my family.

It might be a good thing to work in the church nursery or in the school lunchroom every week, but sometimes we may have to say no because we need that time to care for the needs of our own families in a more relaxed way.

Delegating some of my responsibilities. I like things done well. Once, when I was going crazy trying to keep my large family in line and the house in order, a friend of mine said, "If a job is worth doing, it is worth doing poorly."

Say that again?

I had to think about her comment for a moment, then I reluctantly agreed. Even if it's not done the precise way I would have done it, the important thing is that the job gets done. Maybe the laundry isn't folded the way I would have folded it, but my eighteen-year-old son does a pretty good job.

Keeping my eye on the family's state of fun and humor. When I don't hear laughter in our home, I get concerned. Laughing and having fun together is so important to our family. Many a tense situation is eased with humor. I have discovered the importance of being able to laugh at myself or the situation, even a difficult situation. And I try not to take myself or life too seriously. One of the greatest blessings in our earthly pilgrimage is a good sense of humor.

Leaving room in my day and on my calendar for the unexpected. Is your schedule so full that one "unexpected" event messes up your whole day? My daily schedule is usually so crammed that a sick child or even a phone call can put me far enough behind to have to play catch-up for the rest of the day.

But I'm learning.

The other day I had plans to accomplish a few tasks around the house before heading out for a couple of afternoon appointments. The phone rang, and I heard the small voice of my granddaughter say, "Mama G, I miss you. Can I come over to your house?"

"Of course, honey," I answered. I left the household chores, postponed my appointments, and spent the day with two of my grandchildren. What a fun, wonderful day I had! And I could have so easily missed it.

Learning to relax. For me, the emphasis is on the word *learn.* I have to make myself relax because my tendency is to feel that being still or having an unoccupied hour is almost a sin. I can't even enjoy relaxing in my yard because I soon see all the weeds that need pulling or the cobwebs that need removing, so I get up and go to work.

I envy those who either don't see dirt and weeds, or don't care. Slowly, little by little, I am learning to follow their example, learning that it really won't make that much difference if I wait till next week to pull the weeds, and that probably no one but me will notice the silky spider webs dangling from the rafters.

The trade-off? An hour sitting in my yard savoring the scent of jasmine blossoms and listening to the wind blowing through the pine branches while watching the giant blue heron walk slowly, silently across the grass—all of which I would have missed if I hadn't taken the time just to sit. I remember the verse that says the Lord has given me "richly all things to enjoy" (1 Timothy 6:17 KJV), and I wonder how many of them I've missed because I've been too busy to notice them.

Seeking help. If you find yourself so frazzled that you're experiencing depression, anger, loss of sleep, or anxiety, maybe you're in need of help—physical help or emotional help. Don't hesitate to seek it. Many people—especially Christians—wait too long to seek help for the problems they face. They would rather "maintain an image" than work on their problems. But this only makes things worse. The Lord instructs us to seek help from Him and from each other. We are to carry one another's burdens and help ease each other's loads.

Are your nerves frayed? Are you feeling fragmented and frustrated? Maybe you too just need to sit in your yard or in a big overstuffed chair or go for a walk and take inventory. Consider the choices, think about the trade-offs, and make the necessary, possibly difficult, decisions that will better enable you to manage your levels of tension and stress.

It's time to un-frazzle your life.

The Choice

$\mathcal{S}$

*E*motion flooded me when the young bride, clutching tightly to her father's arm, entered the church and began to walk slowly down the aisle toward her groom. Tears of joy stung my eyes as I looked at the radiant face of her mother watching them approach the altar.

As the minister began to welcome the guests, my mind wandered back to another emotion-filled day, three years earlier. It was early one morning when the telephone rang and I heard Mary's troubled voice asking if she could come over.

A few minutes later, sitting together on the sofa, she tearfully told me that her only child, Amy, was pregnant. Mary was overcome with distress and confusion. Coming from a large Spanish family and strong Catholic background she had often said in her charming accented voice, "If my daughter ever comes home pregnant, I will strangle her. Then I will leave town. I could never face my family or friends."

Now her worst fears had come true. It was a bad dream that would not go away. After crying together, we prayed, committing every aspect of the situation to the Lord.

Over the next few months, I watched as a special drama unfolded. Amy, a senior at a large state university, at first considered abortion. It was socially and legally "acceptable"—and certainly seemed the easiest way out. So she visited a women's clinic that performed abortions. After having the procedure explained to her, however, Amy knew deep in her heart that abortion could not be an option.

The baby's father offered to marry Amy, but she was unwilling to enter marriage without the full assurance that the decision was based on love—not pity or duty. So she returned to her dorm and carried her child as well as her heavy academic load with courage.

Her mother prayed and trusted God through the many difficult, stress-filled days ahead. With His help, taking one day at a time, she faced her friends and family with dignity.

The months passed quickly, and soon Mary received a call. Amy had delivered a baby girl. While in the hospital, she received a lovely bouquet of flowers. The card read, "Congratulations on the birth of your daughter," and it was signed by the women's clinic where Amy had sought information about abortion.

Upon hearing this, I was humbled. I thought to myself, *Gigi, we who are strong advocates of life had better be careful to show at least as much love and support as this abortion clinic did.*

Although I truly respect those who demonstrate against taking the life of an unborn child, it hurts to see even well-meaning zealots shout insults and try to embarrass and intimidate those who seek counsel from these clinics. If we who are pro-life are going to have a vital influence in our nation on this crucial issue, we must give practical love and support to these needy women rather than humiliating or judging them.

After graduation, Amy returned to her parents' home, found a job, and cared for her child. Through hard work and commitment to her daughter, she continued to earn the respect of both families and of all who knew her. Her child's father continued to court Amy, and soon it was obvious that there was not only respect and admiration between these two, but genuine love as well.

As I sat in the church and witnessed the joining of their lives in marriage, I could only close my eyes and praise the faithfulness of God. When the pastor asked, "Who gives this woman to be married to this man?" the bride's father replied "Her mother and I do." But I also imagined I heard a tiny little girl's voice reply, "Me too."

Those of us who are against abortion may cringe at the word "choice" we hear so frequently these days. But the truth is, God is the author and giver of choices in our lives.

Consider the Garden of Eden. God created the earth and formed a man and a woman to share it with Him. Then He did what seems on the surface a rather strange thing. He placed a tree in the middle of the garden, the tree of the knowledge of good and evil, and told the man and the woman not to eat the fruit of this tree.

Why did He do that? Why did God create such a tree? Why would He place this tree in the garden? Wasn't He offering a true choice to His creatures? He longs for men and women to freely choose to love and obey Him and follow His laws and His precepts. Through the mouth of Moses, God says, "I have set before you life and death...therefore choose life." (Deuteronomy 30:19 NKJV).

Life is holy to God. All through Scripture, life is considered a precious gift from the Creator. Our Lord offers us both earthly and eternal life, but He also gives us another gift…the gift of choice. Just as we can accept or refuse His gifts, we can also abuse them. Yet God holds us strictly responsible for the choices set before us, and we must be willing to bear the consequences of those decisions.

As I listened to the pastor exhorting these young lovers to make good decisions and wise choices and to stay committed to God and to each other, I thought what a valuable lesson this whole experience had taught me. I found myself longing to put my arms around the woman considering an abortion. I found myself wanting to tell her that her Creator and God loves her very much, that He understands her situation better than she will ever realize, and that He longs to help her.

I asked myself, "What would Jesus do if He were standing outside one of these clinics with a woman contemplating an abortion?"

In my mind's eye, I saw Him gently slip His arm around her frail, stooped shoulders and quietly say, "Come with me, you who are carrying this burden, and I will help you find a better way." I also saw Him embrace the woman who had chosen abortion in her past and now carries a crushing load of guilt. I could hear Him say, "My daughter, there is no need to carry this burden any longer. I have paid the price for your sin with My own blood. I stand ready to forgive and to forget your past. All you have to do is ask."

You see, choosing Him is choosing life.

Storm Watch

∽

We all sat huddled together in the family room…waiting…emotionally and physically exhausted.

We'd done all we could do. We'd moved the furniture away from the windows, taped up the glass, retrieved any loose objects from the lawn. We'd spent hours standing in line at the grocery and discount stores purchasing emergency supplies: candles, batteries, drinking water, and canned food (we almost forgot the manual can opener).

We filled the bathtubs with water and made sure the cars were filled with gas. We tuned the TV to the weather channel, which kept us posted every few minutes about the movements of the major storm rapidly approaching our area.

I took a last-minute walk around the yard. It looked so beautiful, so peaceful. The bougainvillea was in full bloom, and the hibiscus blossoms were a riot of color. It felt so strange. There were no visible signs that a terrifying storm was only a few miles off the coast of Fort Lauderdale. The sky overhead was clear and blue. It was a lovely day.

The only difference was an eerie stillness.

No birds chirped in the ficus trees. No dogs barked. No breeze stirred the palm fronds. Somehow nature seemed to sense the proximity of a killer storm. In just a few hours, all this beauty and stillness would be turned into chaos.

I thought about how often I walk serenely through the sunny, cloudless days of my life, completely unaware of the storms lurking just beyond. Yet we will all face storms along the way. Some will be minor, like the everyday gusts that blow through our routine days. Others will be devastating—the death of a loved one, the loss of a job, the discovery of a serious illness—leaving damage and destruction in their wake. Some storms are to be expected, and we can prepare for them to a certain extent. But others are so sudden. Everything is calm, then suddenly we find ourselves overtaken in a raging tempest.

As I walked slowly back inside to wait for the pending storm, I asked myself, *Am I preparing myself and my family for the inevitable storms of life? Am I storing up for the day of adversity? What can we do to help prepare and protect our family?*

In this case we prepared, and we waited. The director of the hurricane center said the hurricane would hit our area around two or three in the morning. We went to bed and awoke at seven.

This time, the storm had miraculously passed us by. Next time, it might descend in all its fury.

But by God's grace, we will be ready.

A Christmas to Remember

∽

I had spent days preparing and packing for all ten of us to make this trip. At the airport, while Stephan went to check in, I tried to keep track of the children plus all the coats and sweaters that would be needed at our destination—but were seldom worn in South Florida.

Finally we boarded the plane.

It was difficult to contain the children's excitement. They bounced around in their seats and argued over who would sit by the window next. We did make it through dinner, however, without a major mishap. Afterward, the flight attendants, dressed as Santas, passed through the cabin with candies, wishing each one "Merry Christmas."

Eventually exhaustion overwhelmed the excitement, and the children fell asleep. *What an unusual way to celebrate Christmas Eve,* I thought to myself. The jumbo jet rushed through the night skies en route to Victoria, British Columbia, where we would visit with Stephan's family.

The plane was virtually empty, so I had room to stretch out, alone with my thoughts. Placing the small Walkman earphones in my ears, I listened to the Christmas carol cassettes I had slipped into my carry-on bag at the last minute. Soon their beautiful, familiar strains filled my whole being with the wonder of this special season.

I looked down upon the earth thirty-six-thousand feet below and watched one small snow-covered town after another pass beneath us. The lights twinkled and glistened off the snow, and I wondered how those people were celebrating this night.

As I've mentioned, I'm usually frantic on Christmas Eve. I sit on the floor wrapping gifts until late, asking myself, *Have I done everything? Will the children be disappointed? Is the turkey defrosted? Did I make enough pies? Where are the stockings? How am I going to convince Stephan to put together one more toy?*

If Stephan were to ask me what I most wanted for Christmas, I would likely reply, "Peace and quiet."

And now I had it.

Gazing at the towns and hamlets gliding by below, I wondered how many others felt as I did on most Christmas Eves. Were they rushing around now doing last-minute shopping, frayed and frustrated because the toy store failed to get another shipment of the latest children's craze? Were they dreading disappointment on Christmas morning? Were they worn out? Harried? Did they long for a good night of rest and a day of peace and quiet?

As the majestic music continued to soothe my soul, I prayed for those below, beleaguered by their blessings. Just before we landed, I woke the children. Quickly gathering our belongings and stuffing ourselves into coats and jackets, we hurried to greet family members we hadn't seen for some time, then made our way to the hotel.

It was late when finally I tucked each small child into bed, making sure he or she was warm enough. Later, as I lay recuperating in a warm bath, I reflected on the fact that although I was tired and weary I was not completely worn out. I was fatigued but not utterly frazzled. I wondered why. Could it be that, in spite of everything, this Christmas Eve was simpler?

I pulled on a warm robe and went to look out the window. What a charming town. So different from South Florida, where we celebrate Christmas in sundresses and sandals and decorate palm trees instead of evergreens.

I opened the window, careful not to wake Stephan, and felt the cold, fresh air rush in. Then I crawled between crisp, white sheets and, with a thankful heart, fell asleep.

On Christmas morning I awoke to the smell of fresh coffee. A moment or two later, Stephan entered our room with a steaming cup and a cheery "Christmas gift!" (We follow an old family tradition of seeing who can be the first to say "Christmas gift" on Christmas morning.) We dressed and went down to breakfast; soon our tummies were satisfied.

I decided to take the children off to explore the town. It was a glorious Christmas Day. It definitely felt cold for us thin-blooded Floridians, but the sun was bright and the sky brilliant blue.

We walked along the port, watching the boats bobbing in the gentle waves. We passed the Parliament building and the museum. We glanced through the doorways of cozy tea rooms and peeked into cleverly decorated shop windows. We walked up and down the small, quaint streets, wondering how those behind the doors of the charming cottages were celebrating this Christmas morning.

Soon we came upon a large, picturesque hotel that dominated one side of the port. Beginning to feel the bite of cold air, we decided to go in and investigate. Instructing the children to behave and reminding them of their manners, I shepherded them into the lobby. I heard music and noticed people assembling in front of the large fireplace. I quickly found a big winged chair, sat down, and gathered the children around me.

Suddenly an ensemble of men and women dressed in historical costumes walked into the room. They began to sing Christmas carols, and for over half an hour, they sang one familiar favorite after another. Sitting there before the open fire, surrounded by all my children and listening to carols on this special morning, I was overcome by emotion.

For me *this* was Christmas.

No hustle and bustle, no hurry and haste, no stress and strains, no fruitless frustrations. Just warmth, love, family, and a quiet, peaceful heart overflowing with gratefulness. What more could a mother ask for?

All too soon the singing was over, and we found ourselves once again bundling up against the cold. It was nearly time for lunch, so we made our way back to our hotel. Over hot soup, thick bread, and tangy cider, sharing our discoveries with Stephan, I experienced a warm sense of contentment.

The afternoon passed quickly, and we hurried to ready ourselves for Christmas celebrations with Stephan's family. Soon all ten of us joined all ten of them in their apartment for a delightful (if some-times noisy) evening.

Because they were not yet in their new home, Stephan's parents had kept things simple: a simple tree, a simple meal, and simple gifts. But we made up for it with lots of happy chatter and confusion.

I sat on the end of the sofa, observing the joyful chaos, watch-ing everyone laugh at the antics of our toddler. I listened to all the aunts and uncles talking with our teenagers. I looked at Stephan's elderly father and mother simply enjoying the happy commotion of being surrounded by their large family. I noticed how much the chil-dren were reveling in all the love, attention, and acceptance of the extended family. I saw Stephan observing it all and glimpsed the parental pride in his eyes.

We ate dinner, opened our few gifts, then gathered to share the Christmas story. "For unto you is born this day in the city of David a Saviour, which is Christ the Lord" (Luke 2:11 KJV). *This is the often-forgotten treasure,* I thought. *Simply that we have a Savior.*

Later that night while tucking each child into bed, I thanked the Lord for reminding me again that the real celebration of His birth is not in the temporary pleasure found in the tinsel and toys...nor in the transient satisfaction of lovely gifts...nor in the brief display of magnificent decorations...nor in the fleeting enjoyment of delicious food.

The real meaning of Christmas is found, not in the ephemeral, but in the eternal.

Why do I forget this year after year? Why is it that I usually think of Christmas with dread? Surely this was not the way it was meant to be.

True Christmas was more like what I had experienced that day: love and sharing, being together and doing for others, finding joy in giving to Him the gift of ourselves.

In the still darkness of the night I thought, *I must try to understand just why Christmas has become so chaotic for me.*

Could I be too caught up in the expectations of others? Am I afraid of disappointing or letting someone down? Are others *really* expecting so much of me, or am I imposing these expectations and pressures on my perfectionist self?

One way I could begin to cope and change would be to deliberately decide not to try to fulfill each wish and expectation. I could choose two or three pressures that I would determine to eliminate. Would my friends really be offended if they didn't receive a Christmas card this year? Maybe I could send Easter cards instead.

Would the children really be disappointed if we gave fewer gifts or decorated a smaller tree? Would the neighbors truly mind if I gave them a small ornament instead of a bag of home-baked goodies?

I don't want to dampen all the traditions and expectations of the holiday season, but I do want to make sure my priorities are in the right order. I want time to think about the real meaning of Christmas, time to concentrate my energy and efforts on people in the community and their concerns…instead of tinsel and temporal things.

Decorations and festivities are wonderful ways to commemorate the birth of a loved one, but I thought how terribly hurt I would be if on my birthday everyone was so busy getting ready to celebrate that no one remembered me.

Surely the Lord, too, must enjoy the time we spend with Him. Time alone in quiet meditation, time together in worshipful praise and thanksgiving.

I soon fell asleep with praise on my lips and thanksgiving in my heart for all that this special Christmas had brought to me. Somewhere beneath all the temporal trappings, the true, timeless treasure still waits to be found.

Come…and behold Him!

Unwelcome News

❦

*L*isa and I were watching her three young children—my grandchildren—scramble up the side of the steep hill in front of us as we walked together to church.

"Why do children prefer to climb the hill and get dirt and grass stains all over their Sunday clothes instead of walking up the stairs?" she wondered.

I laughed. "I guess it's the same reason a little boy will invariably try to balance himself on the edge of the curb instead of staying on the sidewalk—or the same reason he walks along the top of every wall he sees, no matter how high."

Looking at them, my grateful heart whispered, *Thank You, Lord, for these precious little ones.*

Suddenly Lisa said, "Gigi, I need you to pray for me this coming Tuesday."

"Of course," I replied, "but why? Is there any special reason?"

"Well," she said, "I have a doctor's appointment."

My eyes lit up with joyful expectation. "Could it be another grandbaby?" I asked.

"No," she replied quietly. "They found a lump."

My heart seemed to stop beating for a moment. I felt cold—then hot all over. *Oh no, Lord, not Lisa!*

My mind raced back several years. Lisa's only sister, Julie, had also discovered a lump in her breast, and after many long months of treatment...hope...more treatment...then bitter disappointment, she died at the age of thirty-one. Neither of us missed the fact that Lisa was now thirty-one.[1]

We continued walking up the sidewalk, but what had been a beautiful, happy Sunday was suddenly overshadowed by deep dread and apprehension.

I slipped into the pew beside my husband, and the grandchildren snuggled around us. After a few moments, I leaned over and told him what Lisa had shared with me.

Immediately, tears filled his eyes. I tried not to show it, but all during the service, every time I looked at Lisa and my son or whenever one of their children climbed up into my lap, a sick, sinking feeling overwhelmed me.

It was difficult to fall asleep that night, and the following morning when I awoke, it hit me all over again...the cold then hot sensations...the nausea...all the emotions that accompany anxiety, fear, and dread. I reproached myself. *Why can't I simply trust that the Lord is in control?*

I understood in my head and knew in my heart that my loving heavenly Father was in control. But my emotions just didn't want to fall in line.

We all will experience times when a phone call, a letter, or a knock at the door will bring sudden, unwelcome, unwanted news. And although we know this is part of life, it doesn't make it any easier when it comes.

How are we to react to unwelcome news? What do we do with our questions, anxieties, and fears?

Each time I encounter a valley in my life, I turn to the Book of Psalms. It's almost automatic, I love them so. And as I've read, I've often wondered just how different those psalms would have been if the psalmist had not allowed himself to feel his emotions. So many of the beautiful passages that offer such strength, courage, and comfort during difficult times would be missing.

David had deep feelings, and he was honest with his emotions. He questioned, he agonized, he became angry; he was despondent and depressed. He often admitted that his spirit was overwhelmed and his heart was desolate. He lamented his circumstances and agonized over his sins.

But David never lost sight of who God is...that God is love and that He is ultimately in control. David knew that God not only sees each tear but cares enough to collect them and put them in a bottle (Psalm 56:8 KJV). David offers us a picture of a tender, caring heavenly Father who will never cause His child a needless tear.

Upon receiving the news that his own son was trying to kill him, David said, "You are a shield around me, O LORD; you bestow glory on me and lift up my head" (Psalm 3:3). Again and again David concluded that God is worthy to be praised even during the most trying times.

One of the great saints said, "Faith sees a smile in God's eyes even when His face frowns." There are times in my life when I think God must be frowning on me. Otherwise why would He allow me to experience this particular pain? Why would He allow this hardship or disappointment? But faith looks beyond...into His eyes...and although we may not understand now, faith sees love in those eyes.

As I heard someone say recently, "When you can't see God's hand, just keep trusting His heart."

I thought I heard the Lord say, "Gigi, when unwelcome, unwanted news comes knocking at the door of your life, don't be afraid to feel your emotions but focus your faith on Me and My faithfulness...not on the trials or circumstances."

Tuesday arrived, surgery was scheduled, and our fears intensified. Because of a prior commitment, I had to go out of town the day of surgery. Fear and anxiety accompanied me all the way to the airport.

Suddenly the car phone rang. Apprehensively, almost reluctantly, I answered.

"It was benign!" my husband exclaimed. "Absolutely no trace of cancer! Have a wonderful trip, honey."

I bowed my heart. *Oh, thank You, Lord! Thank You!*

"Oh for grace to trust Him more!"

Protecting Those
Little White Squares

∽

*T*he alarm clock suddenly jangled me out of sleep.

Ever so reluctantly, I disengaged myself from the comfort of my bed and groped my way down the hall toward the kitchen. The children gradually emerged from their bedrooms in various stages of dress. Forty hectic minutes later I waved good-bye to the last child, closed the front door, and sat down with a cup of coffee.

It was hard to believe that the lazy, laid-back days of summer were over and the new school year had begun. I picked up my calendar. Already those little white squares, the building blocks of the months, had begun to fill with school activities, sports schedules, social obligations, doctor appointments, and church events.

There on one square was my birthday. Others were occupied with a trip to the West Coast, Antony's birthday, then Berdjette's. Neon yellow circled writing deadlines, and out-of-town obligations stretched across several days.

I stared at the calendar in dismay. What had happened to my fall? How had it all crept up on me so quickly?

Each year I vow to carefully control my schedule, as well as my family's, so we won't find ourselves in this very situation. But all too soon the days are choked with deadlines and obligations. The little squares fill up with scribbles, times, and penciled duties...which leaves precious little room for the many unexpected, unplanned, or "Oh-mom-I-forgot-to-tell-you" things that inevitably come along.

I have a feeling I'm not alone in this frustration.

Most families I know can identify with the queen in *Alice in Wonderland,* who said, "I have to run as fast as I can just to stay in place, and if I want to get anywhere I have to run twice as fast as that."

Many families seldom eat dinner together, much less spend an evening watching a favorite TV show together or playing a game or just talking to one another. Often the only time families have "together" at all is in the car on the way to an activity.

I don't think family life has to be this way. There are specific, practical things we can do to avoid being so busy and living such hectic lives. But those things require determination and cooperation.

Perhaps as families we should sit down with our calendars and take a good look at the different things in which we're involved. Together, we can determine which commitments represent things of lasting value and which could be eliminated. Dad's and Mom's work responsibilities will have to take precedence over many other activities, but even these should be evaluated.

Recently, a highly paid sports announcer from a large city shocked his audience by announcing his resignation. His reason? He wanted more time with his family. Stepping away from the hot television lights, he took a lower paying, less demanding public relations job—and found more time to play baseball with his little boy.

Sports and after-school activities afford excellent opportunities for young people, but some parents sign up their children for every-thing. I have friends who spend most of their time driving their children from one activity to another, grabbing a hamburger on the way. If we're not careful, we'll find ourselves exhausted, spending our valuable time chauffeuring instead of parenting.

Church involvements should undergo the same scrutiny. While I firmly believe families should plug into a good, Bible-teaching church, some families feel compelled to be in church several times a week. I remember one father of six, the headmaster of a Christian school, telling me, "One of the biggest mistakes I made as a parent was to believe that my children had to be in church every time the doors were open."

Perhaps we could choose carefully as a family the areas of church we wish to participate in besides the Sunday morning worship service. When I was a child, our church didn't offer Sunday evening services. So each Sunday evening, my grandparents came over for a "pickup" supper. Then we sat around the living room, singing hymns and playing Bible games. Most of the Bible truths I learned and many of my warmest childhood memories stem from those special Sunday evenings.

Many older children hold after-school jobs that teach them responsibility and the value of money. But employment shouldn't rob a child of valuable family time or take the place of his or her chores at home. Some of our family memory-building times are spent working together in the yard: raking leaves, then jumping into the pile, trimming bushes, making trips to the dump, washing the cars, getting soaked fixing the sprinkler heads, even cleaning closets.

Being too busy has become a compulsion, a way of life for most families. And we really need to be careful. Someone once said, "If the devil can't make you bad, he makes you busy." The family *is* under attack today. Satan is doing his best to undermine and undo the home, and I believe one of his favorite strategies is to simply get us all too busy. When we are tense and tired and overextended, we begin to forget those things that are truly important.

As we analyze and re-evaluate our schedules, let us "trust in the LORD with all [our] heart and lean not on [our] own understanding; in all [our] ways acknowledge him, and he will make [our] paths straight" (Proverbs 3:5–6).

Before you start marking up those clean little white squares on the calendar, it's good to remember that every one of them belongs to Him.

No Wasted Pieces

∾

A tourist strolling through a European village stopped to observe a master craftsman of gold filigreed porcelain.

He watched as the craftsman took one of his loveliest pieces, an exquisite vase, and carefully examined it. After a few minutes, a faint smile of satisfaction touched the corners of the artist's mouth.

The workmanship was perfect. The size and form were just right; the artwork, intricate and delicate. Then, to the horror of the tourist, the craftsman picked up a hammer and smashed it into a thousand pieces.

"Why?" cried the stunned man when he finally retrieved his breath. "Why did you do that?"

The craftsman looked at the tourist and explained. "You see, my friend," he said, "the value of this vase is not in its perfection. Not in the artwork, not in its form or shape—as lovely as these may be. No, the value lies in the fact that I am now going to put these pieces back together again. With gold!"

So it is with our lives. The value of our lives lies not in our perceived perfections or lack of them…not in what we've done or left undone…not in how hard we've worked…not in our efforts, as sincere as they may be…not in the hope that we'll get a second chance to redeem ourselves. No, the value of our lives lies in the fact that *God wastes nothing.* He takes all the pieces of our lives, even the imperfect, shattered fragments, and puts them back together again with His blood, which is infinitely more precious than gold.

This story reminds me of a wonderful little verse of Scripture found after the account of the feeding of the four thousand. Jesus tells His disciples, "Gather the pieces that are left over. Let nothing be wasted" (John 6:12).

What encouragement this is to me. God never wastes the suffering or brokenness, nor the faults and failures of His children. With God there are no broken pieces of our lives lying around, discarded and wasted.

Master Craftsman that He is, He knows how to redeem every fragment. And use them all for His glory.

I Wasn't Prepared
for a Prodigal

❧

I stood in the doorway, watching my son walk slowly down the drive-way and out into the street. Then, with a heart that felt heavy as lead, I reluctantly turned away.

I forced myself to go through the motions of fixing dinner and doing the evening chores. When I finally crawled into bed, I lay awake, crying and wondering. Where was he? Had he eaten supper? Did he have a place to sleep? Could we have done things differently? *Would he ever come home again?*

I thought back over the past months. The ups and downs, the emotions, the harsh words, the frustrations, the disobedience, the dishonesty, the questions, the long nights...sitting and waiting, wondering, worrying, asking, "Why?"

Why was our son choosing to rebel against all we'd offered him? A warm, loving home, physical comfort, an education, a godly heritage. We had wanted him, prayed for him, and had been overjoyed at his arrival. He had been such a fun-loving, happy child. We called him our "sunshine."

Unable to control the tears, I thought about all the chances we had given our son. We had taken him back again and again only to have him abuse our trust and disrupt our family life. We had done all we knew to do until finally, tonight, because of the other children, my husband had to ask him to leave our home.

I wasn't prepared for a prodigal. I never imagined I would one night lie in bed, wondering where my son was. But once you love, you are never free again, and the Lord caused this heartbreaking situation to teach me many things. I have had to cope with overwhelming sadness that at times almost engulfs me.

After years of our giving all we had to this beloved child, he chose to disregard his training and reject his teaching. But as painful as it was, Stephan and I also realized we could not allow the behavior of this one child to consume us. At times we've had to purposefully put our prodigal out of our minds. It simply wasn't fair to focus all our attention and emotional energy on him at the expense of the other members of the family.

I have also had to deal with guilt.

During the first few months and many times afterward, I experienced searing stabs of guilt and self-doubt. Could I have brought him up differently? Had I been too strict—or not strict enough? Had I shown enough love? Had I truly gone the extra mile?

I know I made mistakes, but I also know I did my best. So I had to recognize these stabs of guilt for what they were: attacks of Satan to discourage and paralyze me. At times the Lord had to gently remind me to deal with my son as He deals with His children: to keep the doors of communication always open, to accept the person, even when I could not accept his actions and conduct.

Sometimes accomplishing this was terribly difficult. I had to ask the Lord for His wisdom and discernment in knowing how to demonstrate love to my son without approving of his behavior. The Lord reminded me that sometimes love has to be tough. Sometimes lessons are only learned the hard way. So I also had to be careful not to interfere with God's dealings in my son's life, allowing him to suffer the consequences of his choices and actions—even though my mother's heart wanted to shield him.

I also had to deal with repeated disappointment. My emotions felt as if they'd been jerked along on a carnival ride. Up. Down. High. Low. Soaring. Crashing. From time to time the situation seemed improved, the tensions less, my son's attitude different. I was encouraged, and my hopes rose—hopes that he would keep his job, go back to school, be sorry, change his ways, even come home again. But soon we would experience yet another disappointment.

But the Lord is the Author of hope. The greatest lesson I had to learn was to release my white-knuckle grip and allow God to be in control of these circumstances. The Lord wants us to be totally dependent on Him every minute of every day, and He chose this situation in my life to teach me once again that He is able.

Stephan says that patience is faith seeing the finished product. Andrew Wyeth, the American artist, once said the most irritating experience for an artist is to have his work criticized before it is finished. If you have a prodigal—a son, daughter, husband or father, a mother or wife who is wandering spiritually, be persistent in prayer and be patient. And be encouraged! Remember, God is not finished.

Two poems written March 7, 1989, the night Tullian left home.

I sit and wait…wondering…
My child is late.
And my mother's heart is worried.

All is quiet…all is still.
All but my anxious heart.
And as my eyes fill up and spill the tears
Upon my upturned face,
I ask, "Lord, give me grace."

∽

Lord, bring him back.
Please bring him back
into this land again.
But while he is away
With him closely stay.
And bring peace to my troubled heart.
Let the tears that start
Each day to flow
Be turned into a prayer
Because I do not know
What to do…Where to start!
Lord, please take
A worried mother's heart
As an offering today
And bring my boy home to stay.

BASED ON JEREMIAH 31:16–17

P. S. Tullian's story has a happy ending. Keep reading!

PART THREE

Quiet Pools

∽

*"And when the storm is all passed,
the brightness for which He is preparing us
will shine out unclouded.
And it will be Himself."*

MOTHER GRAHAM

(MY GRANDMOTHER)

The Keeper

$\backsim$

*A*flood of gratitude engulfed me as I sat behind my handsome young son. His arm draped around the shoulders of his beautiful fiancée as they listened to the words of the song "The Keeper." He too was having a difficult time holding back the tears.

Just five years before I had wondered if I would see this beloved son again. Tullian[1] was our prodigal. His father and I had given him all we could. We loved him dearly, but he chose to disregard his teaching and training and turn his back on all that we offered. So we had no choice but to let him go—at sixteen.

Although there was really nothing else I could do during that troubled time, I often found it difficult to trust the Lord. I found myself wondering, *Why did God give this boy parents if He didn't want us to be in charge?* So I would try my best to do something—anything—to help God. I would interfere, manipulate, scheme, and even try to control the situation. My mother's heart ached for him. I wanted to protect him.

It didn't help. It only frustrated me and fragmented the family. I finally understood that if God was going to work, I had to get out of His way. I had to accept the fact that God loved my son even more than I did. When I accepted this, I was able to turn him loose. I was able to surrender Tullian, really surrender him, to the Lord. I would continue to do the possible, but I would let God handle the impossible.

As the years came and went, however, I often found myself discouraged. My hopes would build, only to come crashing down in bitter disappointment. I was tempted again and again to try to do God's job for Him. Then I would cry the words of the old hymn, "Oh for grace to trust Him more!" And in response I would hear a still, small voice deep within my heart saying, "Love and patience...love and patience."

My daddy would call every week and ask, "How is Tullian?" Then he too would echo the words I had heard in my heart, "Love and patience...love and patience."

I didn't have a problem with the love part. After all, I'm a mother. But I had a lot of trouble with the patience. My mother reminded me that in dealing with an all-knowing, all-loving, all-powerful God, I had not only to pray with persistence but with patience.

The Lord showed me a delightful verse tucked deep in the book of Isaiah:

"Therefore will the Lord wait, that he may be gracious unto you.... He will be very gracious." (Isaiah 30:18–19 KJV)

Several years passed. Then, totally unexpectedly, Tullian took his girlfriend by the hand one Sunday, and from high in the balcony of our church, they went forward to give their lives to Jesus Christ.

I was overwhelmed with joy—but also a bit skeptical. I didn't want to have my hopes dashed again. I waited and watched. As the weeks turned into months, we saw this young man grow and mature into a sincere, dedicated child of God.

Recently he wrote to an older Christian friend. I asked him if I could share this excerpt:

> Things went real raw after I last saw you. My whole life went down the tubes. I really fell far from the Lord. Drugs, alcohol, sex, the whole nine yards. I dropped out of school, got kicked out of my house; things couldn't have gotten much worse.
>
> But I don't want to go on about the bad stuff. I want to tell you about what the Lord has done for me. After leading a very empty, up and down lifestyle, I gave the Lord total control of my life. What a change. Things I used to live for don't even matter anymore. Things I used to run away from, I'm hungry for.
>
> Isn't God good? He has been so patient with me. He never gave up on me. For the first time in my life I feel peace and contentment. I don't worry about anything. I am a totally different person.

Yes, our prodigal has returned.

We recently celebrated Tullian's marriage to his lovely Kim; together they're attending a Bible college to prepare themselves for ministry. Gratitude fills my whole being. What a privilege it has been for me, a mother, to stand back, out of God's way, and observe His grace at work.

I realize, of course, that not all mothers, wives, fathers, or husbands who have loved, prayed, and faithfully waited for their prodigals to return will see the answers to their hearts' cries. At least not on this side of eternity. Saint Augustine's mother, Monica, did not live to see her prayers for her wicked son answered. But can you imagine the joy she experienced when she stepped into heaven and was shown all that her son would become and do for his Lord?

God will never disappoint us. Remember, if we have been as faithful as we know how to be here on earth, it will be God's greatest joy to spend all eternity making it up to us.

The song was coming to a close. With thanksgiving in my heart I glanced again at Tullian and Kim sitting in front of me. Snatches of a favorite psalm floated into my mind: *"Truly, the Lord is thy keeper...He does not slumber...He shall preserve thy going out and thy coming in."*

P.S. Here's an update! Today, as I work on this book manuscript, Tullian, Kim, and their toddler, Gabe, play beside me in our backyard pool. They just arrived for two weeks of vacation with us. Tullian serves as a youth minister while he finishes with Bible college. By the way...he's making excellent grades. So take courage, anxious parent, and look up!

The Reminder

‍∽

I glanced anxiously out the window. If the storm didn't let up soon, I was going to be late for dinner.

It had been beautiful until just a few minutes earlier when suddenly the sky darkened and thunder began to rumble in the distance. Then the lightning cracked, and the rain came—large, heavy, slow drops at first. Then the heavens opened, and it began to pour. I would just have to wait till it passed.

I returned to the kitchen and grabbed my dustcloth. (No sense wasting time looking out the window. I could at least dust the hallway while I waited.) Sure enough, it wasn't long before the storm moved on. I grabbed my umbrella—just in case—and jumped in the car.

As I sped along, I admired the late-afternoon sun. The western sky out over the Everglades was bathed in a soft, golden glow. I smiled. As many times as I've watched it happen, it always amazes me how suddenly these vicious tropical storms descend upon us and then, just as quickly, pass on.

Turning east along the freeway, I noticed the dark sky up ahead. Jagged bolts of lightning were fiercely attacking the blackness, and the thunder was so loud I could feel the reverberations. I suddenly realized I was heading right back into the *same* storm.

As the rain began to pelt my car, I glanced in my rearview mirror and saw the sun still shining brightly behind me. I wanted to turn back into the sunshine, but I couldn't. There was no way to turn around, so I continued as the storm quickly closed in around me.

Suddenly in front of me, bright against the blackness, appeared a complete, perfect rainbow. I was so filled with emotion I pulled the car over to the side of the highway and just sat there.

This is so much like my life. I get through some dark storm, get a little taste of sunlight on the other side, and then find myself right in the middle of another tempest—even more vicious than the last one. As the new storm builds, I wish I could turn around and go back. I wonder if I will have the spiritual, physical, and emotional strength to face another difficulty. I question myself, and sometimes I even question God. Why me? Why does He allow so many storms? And why do they sometimes occur so close together?

Each of us encounters storms of one kind or another in life. We experience many different kinds of assaults and attacks. Some may be sudden and savage: an accident, a death, the loss of a job. Some are long-lasting and severe: illness, a rebellious child, financial burdens. Some are like the drip...drip...drip...of a slow drizzle: the mundane chores, trying to stretch an already overburdened budget, arguments, noise, traffic, laundry. Our nerves are stretched dangerously thin.

Yes, I've had my share of storms. Some have been large and frightening, others small and annoying. I seem to just get through one difficult time and think, *Whew, that's over. Now I can enjoy life,* when suddenly, without warning, a telephone call throws me directly into the path of another howling gale. Some storms I can see looming in the distance, and a sense of dread overwhelms me. I don't want to enter into the turbulence! I want to bask in the sun, not deal with another sadistic weather system.

But that stormy late-afternoon alone in the car, the Lord taught me something about dealing with difficulties.

As I drove down our driveway after the storm had swept over our home, I was keenly aware of the sunshine—and valued it so much more than I would have had the entire day been sunny and bright. So it is in my life. After going through a stormy period, I appreciate more fully the serene, calm, restful times. Bad weather makes we wish for the sun; adversity causes me to focus more on the Son. These very difficulties make me more aware of His presence.

That day as I turned east and realized I was heading right back into a frightening storm, the warm glow in my rearview mirror reminded me the sun was still there. The Lord used this image to remind me that although the thick clouds of adversity may obscure His presence, He is still there. Just as Moses discovered many years ago, I too have learned that as I draw close to the "thick darkness," I find God is there (Exodus 20:21 KJV).

When I looked toward the jagged bolts of lightning and felt the rumbling thunder, the rainbow, full and complete, reminded me of the fullness of His presence and the complete faithfulness of His promises. He has promised to lead and guide us, to calm our fears, to supply our needs, to be with us through each and every stormy situation, and never to leave us or forsake us.

Sitting there beside the road with cars zooming past me, I looked at the rainbow and was filled with awe. I realized God had used this incredible storm to remind me once again that He is faithful and true. He who has helped me through each past difficulty will be there to help me through the next one.

Whatever your present storms—when the storm clouds swirl around you, when a bolt of bad news splits your life, when the rumbling thunder of approaching trouble fills you with dread—remember…He is there. Focus on His faithfulness and not on your circumstances. Fill your heart with confidence that He will see you through whatever lies ahead.

The Trouble with Seeds

∽

*H*earing a commotion, I looked up and saw three of my grandchildren running up the front walk.

"Hi, Mama G!" they squealed, throwing their little arms around my neck and planting wet kisses on my cheek. "We love you, Mama G!" they chorused.

My eldest son, who was dropping them off for the night, soon followed with his arms full of "blankies," dolls, and one very necessary pink pacifier. Holding the three little ones in my arms, I watched as my son deposited the various bundles in the entrance hall, kissed us all good-bye, then drove down the road and around the bend. I stood there waving and thanking the Lord for these precious rewards that, as a younger mother, I wondered if I would ever reap.

I held them in my arms...and thought about seeds.

I dislike them.

Every now and then, the children come home from school with a little package of seeds. They ask me to help plant them in a small plastic container so they can watch them grow. The next morning, bright and early, they run to see if the plant has sprouted yet. Immediately they're disappointed. They water the little seed again and the next day repeat the routine. After two or three days with no results, they're ready to throw in the trowel!

I understand.

Waiting patiently for sprouts certainly doesn't appeal to me. I prefer to take our Chevy Blazer down to K-Mart, back up to the garden department, and fill the trunk with full-grown plants, loaded with buds and blooms. I rush home, immediately plant them, and by evening I have an instant, beautiful yard bursting with color.

The trouble is, I often react to my life and my Christian growth the same way. I get discouraged waiting for the blooms.

"Mother, you've been doing the same thing for *so many years!*" my eldest daughter exclaimed recently. She had been watching me clean the kitchen, gather up the dirty clothes, straighten the beds, and make arrangements for the younger children before we could head out the door and go shopping together.

The problem with life is that it's so *daily*. We do the same mundane, monotonous chores every day, week after week, month after month. We repeat the same words for *years:* "Eat your food…brush your teeth…clean your room…pick up your clothes…get off the phone…don't stay out too late."

All of that seed-planting…and we are so seldom rewarded for our efforts. We look expectantly each day to see if our words and instructions have finally taken root, only to experience one disappointment after another.

We straighten one room, only to find it a mess again an hour later. We finish washing the breakfast dishes, only to hear, "Mom, I'm hungry! Can we have a snack?" The children change their clothes two or three times a day, leaving the discarded ones strewn about like vestiges of modern art. Their friends come and go, leaving a trail of grit and grime. The kitchen is never clean, the icemaker is always empty, and paper cups are discarded all over the house and yard.

I had to laugh when I read a piece of wit from the late Erma Bombeck, who said she remembered *how* she got her kids but didn't remember *why*. I have to admit that many times I've wondered why I ever thought I could handle motherhood or be an effective parent. I have made, and continue to make, so many mistakes. I fail more often than I succeed in dealing with the children—especially the teenagers. I get frustrated, lose my patience, and seem to linger in a state of emotional and physical depletion.

Then, just when I think I can't take any more, just at the time I need it most, the Lord rewards me. The grandchildren come running in to hug me, or one of my grown children calls just to say, "Hi, I love you." My son-in-law, studying for his master's degree, sends me a copy of his transcript—all A's. One of the teenagers, seeing me fold laundry, stops and gives me a kiss, and my ten year old remembers to do at least one of his chores without being told.

No longer just seeds, but (finally!) blossoms.

So allow me to offer a little encouragement here—especially to moms. When you get so discouraged you wish you could just give up…when you're so tired you lose patience…when you make mistakes, and begin to ask, *"Why did I ever get into this parenting business?"*…remember this promise from a mother who sees parenthood from both sides now.

Rewards are waiting for you.

And yes, it is more than worth it.

Just be patient, and the seeds you have so faithfully watered will sprout and bloom. For now, enjoy planting and watering your garden. And remember that Jesus said, "Whatever you did for one of the least of these…, you did for me" (Matthew 25:40).

Along the Brick Pathway

⌀

I spent the past week laying brick. By Wednesday I wondered what in the world had ever inspired me to begin such a project.

Thursday morning I was so sore and achy I didn't know if I could get out of bed. I thought I'd caught a flu bug. By Friday, I realized it wasn't the flu. I had simply used muscles that had not been used in a very long time (if ever), and those muscles were protesting in the only way they knew how. Each evening I took a hot bath, crawled into bed, and asked Stephan to please bring me the Tylenol.

When I first asked my friend to teach me to lay bricks, he said, "No problem." It sounded like such a simple project. An afternoon or two at the most. Looking back now, I begin to realize that when my friend said, "No problem," what he *meant* to say was, "Not impossible."

Thirty-three years ago I approached having a child the same way I considered bricklaying. There would be little to it, I thought. A relatively simple project.

When Stephan and I first married, the only thing I wanted was a baby. After a month of marriage when I discovered I was not "with child," I began to cry and pray, thinking I would never have children.

A month after that, I had real hope—but still wasn't sure. I was only seventeen, both Mother and my doctor were on the other side of the world, and I didn't think Stephan knew any more than I did, so I prayed, "Lord, the only thing I know about being pregnant is that women usually experience morning sickness. So, if I am expecting a child, please help me to be sick." The next morning and every morning for the next three months, I was SICK.

This past Tuesday, when my back and I were already having second thoughts about the bricks, I looked at the hardened cement and realized it was too late to retreat. I was committed. Thirty years ago, fighting morning sickness, I also suddenly realized I was committed. A few months later, when my first baby boy was placed in my arms and I looked into his deep blue eyes and examined his tiny fingers and toes, I never dreamed of all the hard work that would have to go into this "project." But I soon discovered that, like laying brick, parenting is permanent.

You can't give up. Once you start it, the job has to be completed.

I began parenting by just starting in. I had no plan, nor did I stop to count the cost of materials or energy. I had no idea of the patience and persistence that would be needed, but I did have a great love of children and a wonderful pattern to follow.

Today I see many young people wisely stopping to "count the cost" before plunging into parenthood. My daughter and her husband are soon expecting their first child. They talked about and planned for this baby, and we all await the birth with joy and anticipation.

But another young woman recently wrote to me, asking for

prayer because she is fearful of taking the step into parenthood. While plans and preparation are important and part of our responsibility in life, we also must remember that we can only plan and prepare so much. A time comes when we must take a step of faith and trust God to provide for the unknown, the unexpected, and the unpredictable.

If Stephan and I had known beforehand all the financial responsibility, the physical and emotional energy required, we probably wouldn't have had our first child, much less the other six. We would have avoided those problems…but we also would have missed the joys, the intimacy of holding our newborn, the feeling of small arms wrapped tightly around our necks, sticky kisses, the refrigerator filled with "I love Mom and Dad" notes, the pride of graduations, and the joys of young love, marriage, and grandchildren.

Maybe the Lord doesn't want us to think too hard and long about parenthood but simply to trust Him. I don't wish to imply irresponsibility, only balance. There may *never* be a perfect time for parenthood. Nor will any of us be perfect parents, raising perfect children. That possibility went out the door in the Garden of Eden.

But as I look at my brick walk, I realize it's the ups and downs, the faults, flaws, and imperfections, that give it charm. And I don't know about you, but I prefer charm to perfection. If I had thought about it a little longer and had known the difficulties, I probably wouldn't have laid the first brick.

But now I'm so glad I did.

Love in Motion

◦⁓◦

*J*erushah slammed the front door and stormed down the hallway toward her room. On her way, she shouted out her frustration.

"When God created woman out of one of Adam's ribs, He must have used the most sensitive one!"

I couldn't help smiling.

At sixteen, Jerushah was just beginning to encounter some of the mystique and challenges of what several books and seminars refer to as our "love language," each human being's unique sensitivities and different ways of expressing and receiving love.

The Christmas holiday season was over, and the big ball in Times Square had dropped to announce the beginning of a new year. Now the stores were decorated with cupids and hearts of all sizes in preparation for the next consumer event, Valentine's Day.

Jerushah's outburst and the overabundance of red hearts and mushy messages have made me stop to consider again what it really means to say…"I love you."

Most Valentine cards I've glanced through express love in terms of a feeling. Even the dictionary's first definition is "a fond or tender feeling; a warm liking."

If love is expressed and/or received on the basis of "feelings," then I'm in big trouble! Why? Because my feelings are so *fickle*. In fact, they're totally untrustworthy. They change with the weather, my hormone levels, whether I've slept well or eaten right, and a dozen different variables.

There are times when I experience warm emotion toward Stephan and really feel "in love" with him. Then there are those times when I'm tired, sick, or just too busy, and I don't feel anything.

I usually feel love and tenderness for my children. That was especially true when they were tiny, helpless babies. But there are other times when I feel nothing but frustration and irritation.

Love, as writers, painters, and poets through the years have discovered, is almost impossible to define. Although I say "I love you" many times a day, I'm not at all sure I really understand the true meaning of the phrase. Nor do I always express love in ways that meet the needs and expectations of those around me.

Most of all, I'm concerned that I'm failing to provide an accurate, adequate example for my children of what it means to love. The more I contemplate it, the more I realize that most of what we see and read about isn't really love at all. Although I haven't begun to comprehend the vastness of this subject, I have come to a few simple conclusions.

Love is obedience to God's Word. I used to feel hypocritical if I showed love to someone when I didn't "feel" it. Then one day a friend of mine set me straight. "Gigi," she said, "that's not hypocrisy. That's obedience." We're instructed throughout Scripture to love.

Love is all about giving. "For God so loved that He gave…" Love continues to give and to do even when it does not feel. In our self-centered society, love is all too often measured by what we get, not by how much we give.

Love is also receiving. Some have a difficult time showing love; others have difficulty accepting it. Both are vital components of healthy relationships. We must willingly give and receive for the circle to be complete.

Love requires sacrifice. "For God so loved the world, that he gave his only begotten Son" (John 3:16 KJV). We may never be asked to sacrifice to this extent, but what about sacrificing our time, our desires, our finances, our comfort zones, our energy? Are we willing to love sacrificially—without acting like a martyr about it?

Love is a decision. We decide to love regardless of our feelings. We love even when we can't approve. When our teenage son chose to live in rebellion against his upbringing and his faith, I remembered something my mother had told me several years earlier. She urged me to deal with my children as God deals with me. God loves me even when I disappoint Him. Knowing this, I could continue to love my son and accept him, even though I could not approve of his lifestyle. It is our responsibility to love…it is God's to change hearts.

Love is a commitment. Love entails a stick-to-it-iveness. The rewards of love are not always immediate, but love doesn't give up. As I've said already, when you once decide to love, you are never free again.

One day when Jerushah was about three we were discussing the subject of love. Suddenly she exclaimed, "Mama, I know what love is. It is the same word as *heart.*"

The Scriptures teach that "God is love" (1 John 4:8, 16). My deepest desire is to express to those around me—especially to my family—a little bit of what is within the heart of God.

Let us love one another as God loves us.

China Roots

∽

The jumbo jet eased into the clouds on its descent. My mother, my two sisters, and I had flown halfway around the world for this special occasion.

We peered eagerly from the windows, catching our first glimpse of Shanghai, China. A light fog blanketed the countryside. Small, gray stone farmhouses dotted green fields. Farmers tilled the soil with wooden plows pulled by large water buffalo. In the rice paddies, bent backs were all that was visible as workers planted each small plant by hand. Others threshed wheat by hand, using the highway as a threshing floor. From the air, the countryside looked softly green and picturesque, resembling the many photographs I'd seen.

The jumbo's tires screeched against the runway. We stepped off the plane and onto Chinese soil for the first time. Yet, in some strange way, my sisters and I felt as though we'd been there before. Something about it seemed familiar.

This was the land of our mother's birth, the land where she had spent the first seventeen years of her life. We climbed into a minivan and began what was to be the first of many thrilling (in more ways than one) rides in China. Our driver had a unique way of zooming through crowded streets at top speed, never letting up on the horn and seldom touching the brakes. Miraculously, we avoided hitting anyone.

As dusk began to settle that first evening, a little maid came in to turn down the beds and pull the drapes in our hotel rooms. I asked her to please leave the curtains open so I could watch the lights come on in the city. But as darkness fell, a heavy blackness cloaked the city, dotted only here and there by a few dim lights. *Fourteen million people and so little light.* I thought of Exodus 10:22, which says, "And there was a thick darkness in all the land" (KJV).

This verse took on even more meaning as we traveled this great country and discovered spiritual, economic, and political darkness.

From Shanghai, we began a trip that took us to more than a dozen cities in eighteen days. Along the way we discovered part of our heritage and were reminded of the faithfulness of God. We began with a two-day trip by train, van, and ferry, crossing the Grand Canal and then heading north to Huai Yin, where our grandparents had served as medical missionaries for more than twenty-five years and where Mother was born.

On Mother's Day, we awoke to glorious sunshine and deep-felt emotions. We toured what is left of the hospital compound where God had done so many miracles and changed so many lives. We met many whose lives had been touched physically and spiritually by the faithful missionaries.

I couldn't keep back the tears as I thought of my grandfather, working tirelessly and unselfishly for these people he loved, even giving them his own blood when needed. But he was quick to point out that although he could help heal their bodies, one day the body would die, so their soul was of much more importance. Then he would tell them of the love of Jesus.

We recalled some of the stories we'd been told as children, stories of God's protection, of His loving care and concern. One Christmas when my aunt was a small child, she asked for doll baby glasses. My grandmother wondered how in the world she would ever be able to fulfill such a request. But the next box to arrive from America contained—you guessed it—a package of doll baby glasses. How touched we were by the tenderness of a loving heavenly Father who cared about a little girl's request way off in China.

We recalled another story of two children, a boy and a girl, who were kidnapped by bandits. It was unheard-of to find such children alive, especially if no ransom was paid. But God's people prayed fervently, and soon the baby boy was found. A few days later it was reported that a woman nearby was nursing two babies that were not twins. In this way the baby girl was also found, fat and healthy.

These and other stories taught us that God cares about the small details of our lives as well as the large, seemingly impossible situations that often confront us.

We visited the small stone house where Mother was born more than seventy years ago. I thought of my grandmother, giving birth in that small room with my grandfather tenderly caring for her. I thought of the years of her faithful teaching and living a personal, vibrant faith. My grandparents provided examples of fun-loving Christians, deeply committed to one another and to their work, and totally dependent upon Almighty God and His grace and mercy.

I longed to be alone with my mother and sisters to allow all of these memories and emotions to flow. But in China, with over a billion people, it is nearly impossible to be alone. So I thought of how often God told the children of Israel to "remember."

"Remember what the LORD thy God did..." and "Remember how the LORD led..." and "Remember the days of old, consider the years of many generations: ask thy father, and...thy elders, and they will tell thee" (Deuteronomy 32:7 KJV).

I came home to America and my family with a new desire and a new determination to be not only as faithful as I can be in my own life but to faithfully tell my children of all that God has done and is doing. I want to remind them, encourage them, and tell them again and again of the faithfulness of God.

In China I was reminded again of Deuteronomy 6:7, which admonishes us to teach our children diligently all that God has taught us and done for us. "You shall teach them...and shall talk of them when you sit in your house, when you walk by the way, when you lie down, and when you rise up" (NKJV).

How important it is to share with our children our own personal scrapbook of the faithfulness of God—the different ways He has led us, provided for us, and sheltered us. Our children need to hear again and again our gratitude to God for His gifts of friends and family and the awesome privilege of freedom. Then they too will come to depend upon Him personally, knowing He will also be ever faithful to them.

Remember...and tell it to your children and your children's children.

Partly Cloudy

∽

I sat outside in the yard looking over the Black Mountain Valley to the gentle Blue Ridge Mountains beyond. I never tire of this view. Ever since I was a young girl, these mountains have given me a sense of serenity.

I heard the familiar creak of the screen door and turned to see Daddy coming out to join me. He sat down in the chair next to mine.

"It sure is a lovely day," I remarked.

"Yes," he replied, "it sure is, but those clouds are building up fast. I'll bet this afternoon there'll be a thunderstorm—and then tomorrow will be overcast."

A few minutes later, Mother also joined us. "It is so nice out here today," Mother exclaimed. "And look at those big beautiful clouds!"

I laughed. So typical. Mother always sees the bright side of life. She sees even the smallest patch of blue sky on a cloudy day, whereas Daddy, like Elijah's servant, tends to see the one small cloud the size of a man's hand in a big blue sky (1 Kings 18:44).

A "partly cloudy" forecast, for people like Daddy, implies bad weather. For others, however, it means a fair and pleasant day. It all depends on how we look at life, what kind of personality we have, or what kind of week we've had.

There are days when "partly cloudy" may mean a reprieve. The heat of some current pressure is obscured for a while by a cloud. Perhaps a change of plans, the cancellation of an appointment, or even the telephone's being out of order for a few hours can offer the refreshing shadow of a free afternoon.

At other times the clouds of disappointment and discouragement can cause a heavy, overcast spirit, sending us into despondency.

The worst kind of "partly cloudy" blocks us from seeing or even feeling the presence of our Lord. The haze of uncertainty interrupts our lives and causes us to stumble.

But remember that clouds are spoken of in Scripture as "the dust of his feet" (Nahum 1:3). In Exodus we read that God came in a thick cloud (19:9) and that the glory of the Lord appeared in a cloud (16:10). When we experience a partly cloudy day, we can be assured that Jesus is walking with us. It is often on these days, when the light is obscured by daily dreariness and mundaneness, that the Lord will appear to us in a special way. Look for Him!

A Brief Blessing

∽

"Fear not, for I am with you;
Be not dismayed, for I am your God.
I will strengthen you,
Yes, I will help you,
I will uphold you with My righteous right hand."

ISAIAH 41:10 NKJV

When I was going through a difficult time, I remembered this brief blessing an older pastor friend had shared with me. In just one verse of just one book of the Bible, we can receive so much help, strength, and encouragement.

In this one verse we have the promise of:

His presence...*I am with you.*

His power...*I will strengthen you.*

His protection...*I will uphold you and help you.*

And these promises are also very personal. Notice the *you.*

"So," this pastor told me, "we can choose to be problem-conscious or power-conscious."

Which are you?

The Barometer

❧

I awoke this morning to clear blue skies. Not a cloud. I love days like this! My mother likes mist and rain, and while I enjoy a cloudy day now and then, over a long period of time the dreariness can depress me.

Some of my friends like cold weather, finding it invigorating and challenging. I don't mind taking a trip to New York or Denver in January. I enjoy bundling up in sweaters and coats that get little use in Florida. But I'm always happy when the plane lands in Fort Lauderdale and I step back into the tropical warmth.

Others love snow and ice. I do too—in pictures or when we're spending a few days in the mountains where I can watch the big flakes float down so softly and hear the snow crunch under my feet. Then, when I've had enough of braving the elements, I can sit by an open fire and sip hot chocolate. But to experience cold for months—to shovel snow day after day—I would find that difficult.

Think for a moment how you feel after a long, cold winter or after a solid week of rain and storms. One morning you draw back your curtains and the fog has lifted, the skies are clear and blue, and the air is gentle and inviting. You feel a sense of exhilaration through and through.

This is how I feel about my life. I like the warm, loving, storm-free days of calm waters and smooth sailing. For most of us, however, reality dictates many days of unsettled weather. There will be days when bad tempers inside the home or office are worse than the afternoon thunderstorm outside, when decisions have to be made and the fog of confusion seems to overwhelm us, or when the constant dripping of complaints causes us to want to scream—or run as fast and far as we can.

One of my greatest desires in life is for serenity. One day I took out a dictionary to see exactly what it was I longed to experience. According to this definition, serenity is "the quality or state of being serene." And what is "serene"? It is "being clear and free from storms, shining bright and steady, and marked by utter calm."

I burst out laughing when I read that. I don't know about you or your home, but ours sure doesn't fit Webster's definition of serene! We seldom go through an entire day "free and clear of storms," and even when we experience a rather peaceful day, it would be going much too far to say it was "marked by utter calm."

Most of our days are filled with stress, pressures, frustrations, and even failures. I awaken to the moans of a child too sick to go to school, and I have to rearrange my whole day. After doing two large loads of wash, the dryer suddenly quits for no apparent reason, leaving me with piles of sopping wet towels and jeans. Writing deadlines are closing in on me or the computer jams, and my already tight schedule is interrupted by countless phone calls. And then, all too soon, the other children arrive home from school, tired, hungry, and arguing with each other and with me over everything. I feel fragmented and frustrated, and I still have dinner to fix and a tired husband to attend to. Eventually I fall into bed, exhausted, dreaming of a "serene" lifestyle.

So often it's the little things that get me down. Sometimes I feel better equipped to deal with major disasters than a steady diet of daily difficulties.

Recently my daughter-in-law told me she was better able to trust the Lord and lean on His strength a few years ago, when her sister was dying of cancer, than she is now with the daily challenges of raising three small children.

How can we experience a measure of serenity in the midst of our hectic lifestyles? I've discovered that when I am at my wit's end, living each day on the ragged edge of exhaustion because of storms of strife and clouds of confusion, I need a "Jesus break." At times like this Isaiah tells us, "Come, my people, enter thou into thy chambers, and shut thy doors about thee: hide thyself as it were for a little moment, until the indignation be overpast" (26:20 KJV).

We need to take a few moments alone with Jesus to unload all our frustrations on Him, to ask Him for His strength, His love, His patience, His wisdom, and to allow the comfort of His understanding and compassion to soothe and calm us.

I'm so thankful the apostle Peter didn't mention size or shape when he said, "Let him have all your worries and cares, for he is always thinking about you and watching everything that concerns you" (1 Peter 5:7 TLB).

Imagine it! Jesus cares about *everything* that concerns us. He cares about all the mundane burdens of our lives: dirty dishes, interruptions, piles of laundry, homework, deadlines, runny noses, demanding bosses, muddy floors, carpools, unpaid bills. Jesus understands our stormy days. Remember, He was the eldest of a large family. I'm sure He experienced His share of daily duties and frustrations.

Yes, most of us prefer bright, steady, calm, storm-free days filled with serenity. For this reason, the Lord has promised not to give us more storms than we can handle. He offers each of us enough serenity in His presence to keep us going moment by moment, one day at a time.

With Him we can shine bright and steady...no matter how the family barometer reads.

What They Need Is a Leader

✧

*F*ive-year-old Stetson listened intently as my daughter-in-law read to him from his Bible storybook. She was reading from the Old Testament about a difficult period in Israel's history.

After hearing of the many spiritual ups and downs, struggles, and failures of God's people, how often they sinned, repented, and then turned around and sinned again, Stetson interrupted his mother.

"Mom, you know what I think?"

"No, honey, what?"

"I think what they need is a *leader*."

As I scan the daily newspaper headlines or watch television or glimpse the latest gossip-grabbers while waiting in line at the check-out counter or listen as my children and their friends discuss their interests and problems, I feel just like little Stetson. What we really need (and cry out for) is leadership.

I read not long ago that experts who deal with children's concerns have declared that they have yet to discover anything better for children than parents. Considering this statement along with Stetson's observation, I thought, *What an awesome responsibility and privilege we parents have to train, direct, and mold the lives of our children!*

The parental leadership role can be a powerful and positive

influence, or it can be abused and become unbelievably destructive.

I was reared by parents and grandparents who, by their loving example and encouragement (and at times their firm discipline), taught me the basic principles of honesty and respect. They offered me direction and guided me into a personal relationship with Jesus Christ and a dependence on God and His Word for guidance and daily strength.

Recently, however, I've been involved in a situation where a Christian parent has abused that privilege of leadership and authority and has caused lasting emotional and physical damage to an entire family.

Leadership is a sacred responsibility. We parents have been placed in positions of leadership, and with this comes a God-loaned authority. How careful we must be not to abuse this trust! If we abuse our authority, we may be in danger of forfeiting our parental privileges.

Some parents take their authority to extremes, causing physical, emotional, and spiritual harm to their children. Others offer no leadership at all for fear of exercising too much control and authority. The children are left to flounder around with little or no guidance.

As I consider the responsibility given to me as a parent-leader, I first have to recognize that I, too, am under authority.

Do you remember the story of the centurion who came to Jesus? He recognized that even Jesus was a Man under authority—the authority of God. When we truly realize and accept this fact, we will acquire a sense of humility, the mark of a true leader.

A real sense of awe envelops me whenever I see leaders (especially men) expressing this humble acknowledgment of need before God. In our church each Sunday the pastor asks the men to come forward and kneel for prayer. I am always moved when I see the leadership of our church on their knees.

As a young girl, I would creep down to my mother's bedroom late at night to ask her a question. Often I would have to wait because she was invariably on her knees in prayer. This left a lasting impression on me and gave me security in knowing I was being prayed for.

The whole concept of leadership for a Christian, and especially a Christian parent, is very different from what we see and hear in the secular world. As a Christian parent-leader we should never lose our servant spirit. We should always be willing to do whatever it takes to get the job done, not caring who gets the credit. We should never place ourselves above others except in carrying more of the responsibility and burdens. We should never lose respect for our children and never think of ourselves as more important than we really are.

We should motivate by example and encouragement, teaching more by the integrity of our lifestyles than by our moral speeches. I'm often reminded of the adage, "What you *are* speaks so loud that your kids can't hear what you say."

Parent-leaders don't have to be authorities on everything, but we should be humble, willing to admit our mistakes, and good listeners. Remember, to be good leaders we don't have to be perfect, but we do have to be real.

Yes, kids need leaders. But what they need most of all is lots of love and lots of encouragement. May God continue to give us the grace, patience, and strength to be leaders for His glory.

The Leaky Hose

∽

I stared at the odd picture above my friend's desk.

At first I couldn't tell what it showed. Suddenly I recognized a long sprinkler hose, the kind filled with tiny holes that allow small jets of water to spray in all directions. Then I noticed the nozzle of the hose lying in the tall blades of green grass with only a lethargic drip or two emerging.

I thought to myself, *This certainly is an unusual picture to find hanging in the office of a renowned psychologist and author—even one with a great sense of humor.*

He noticed my puzzled expression and chuckled. "Do you know why I have that hanging there?" he asked. "To remind me that if I'm not careful to stay focused, my life could become just like that hose."

I laughed, easily identifying with that old hose. I often feel stretched thin...pulled taut...punctured with holes. Frequently I feel pressured to get involved with too many things until my physical, emotional, and even my spiritual energies are dispersed in so many directions that I have nothing left to give but pathetic little drips. I get so busy, so preoccupied with nonessential things, that my mind and body are drained before I get to the truly important things...the things of eternal value.

Most mornings before my feet even hit the floor, the pressure starts to build. It's not that this pressure is all bad. As my mother once remarked, "I don't work well under pressure, but I don't work at all without it." The problem lies in the fact that all the various mundane demands I place upon myself soon diffuse my limited resources.

I regularly fall into bed at night exhausted, feeling as though I've been running and spinning for hours, yet so many things that needed to be done are still undone. I lie there wondering, *What have I really accomplished?*

The other day during my devotions I read the familiar story of Mary and Martha (Luke 10:38–42). On this particular morning, the Lord seemed to speak to me concerning my garden-hose problem through this simple little phrase: "One thing is needful" (v. 42 KJV). Or as another translation reads, "only one dish is needful".

In other words, the Lord seemed to be saying, "Simplify, Gigi, *simplify.*"

As a writer, I appreciate editors. A good editor basically does two things: simplifies and clarifies. And most often, simplifying produces clarity. The editing process isn't always easy. I'm reluctant to cut, condense, or rearrange a piece I've worked on so diligently and wholeheartedly. But it's necessary...if I want quality results.

So it is with my life. I need the touch of a master editor. I work hard, I put my heart into everything I do, I give to a lot of people, I have many responsibilities. And I need help deciding what activities, what expectations, what responsibilities need rearranging, reducing, or even deleting.

My daughter-in-law recently told me that one of the greatest needs she sees today in those around her is the need to simplify their lives. About that same time, the cover story of one of the major weekly newsmagazines was on the nationwide problem of exhaustion. It seems that people from all walks of life are plainly worn out.

This really made me stop and think. I grew up hearing well-meaning people say, "Well, it's better to burn out than to rust out." But is this attitude really pleasing to the Lord? It may sound good, even spiritual, but is it really biblical? I don't think so. As Charles Swindoll once noted, "Burn out or rust out...either way you're *out*."

Maybe we all need to stop, take inventory, and ask ourselves if there is anything we can do to simplify our lifestyles. Maybe we could make parenting a little less complicated, lower the expectations we place upon ourselves and our mates, decrease our wants and wishes, and manage our time and energy more efficiently.

Most evenings in our home are hectic. There is the kitchen to clean, homework to supervise, arguments over the television to negotiate. But a few nights ago after supper, my son and his wife and one of their young friends just sat with us in the family room and talked. The television was turned off, classical music played quietly in the background, and candles flickered on the old coffee table. Later my husband remarked on what a nice evening it had been.

The simple things of life, things we already have, seem to bring us the most pleasure. Gazing at a sunset, feeling a gentle breeze, basking in the warmth of a cozy fire, enjoying the companionship of a good book, holding hands with someone we love, feeling the arms of a child around our necks, hearing the strains of a favorite piece of music. Busier, bigger, or better is rarely best.

We are constantly bombarded with the temptation to be dissatisfied with what we have: our looks, our mates, our homes, our clothes, even the weather. I always have to be on guard against this dissatisfaction. It sneaks up on me, and soon I confuse my needs with my desires. That's when I replace the joy in what I have with longing for what I want.

It has been well said that "wealth consists not in the abundance of our possessions, but in the fewness of our wants."

This could be said also of happiness.

Satisfaction

∽

*S*he is so satisfied with Christ!"

Like a swift dart, this simple remark concerning an older Christian woman went straight to my heart and pierced my conscience.

"Oh!" I thought. "I wish that could be said of me!"

Although I discovered many years ago that Jesus Christ was all I really needed, from time to time I find myself playing the "if-only" game.

I think most of us have at least a passing acquaintance with that little mind game. Sometimes we find ourselves wishing we had a little more: "If only I had more time…more help…more education… more strength…more financial resources…more abilities…more good looks…more rest."

At other times, we find ourselves wishing we had a little less: "If only I had less stress…less responsibility…less work…less kids… less bills…less deadlines…less health problems."

Sometimes the "if-only" game sets us longing for something different: "If only I had a different job…a different home…a different body…a different temperament…a different spouse…a different church…a different spiritual experience…then I'm sure I'd be a happier person."

King David, who knew what it was to live with nothing and to live with everything, recorded this thoughtful prayer for us in one of his psalms:

> But as for me, my contentment is not in wealth but in seeing you and knowing all is well between us. And when I awake in heaven, I will be fully satisfied, for I will see you face to face. (Psalm 17:15 TLB)

Could it be that when we experience those nagging feelings of dissatisfaction or find ourselves playing the "if-only" game, there is something between us and our Lord? Something blocking our relationship with Him?

The Lord tells us through the words of Jeremiah that He "will *fully satisfy* the weary soul...." (Jeremiah 31:25 TAB) The truth is Jesus and *Jesus alone* is the only source of true satisfaction.

Will you pray with me for a moment?

Lord, please bring to light...show me...reveal to me any and all obstacles that keep me from finding my total satisfaction in You. Wean me away from those temporary things that can never really satisfy. Lord, with David I want to tell You that my greatest desire in life is to know that all is well between us. May those who rub shoulders with me this day sense that I am "satisfied with Jesus"...and seek their satisfaction in You, too.

What Can I Take to Heaven?

ⷭ

*A*flood of warm, happy memories flashed through my mind as I passed by the small, white room. I paused a moment in front of the door. What a special joy it is to spend several weeks a year in the little house where I grew up.

Glancing through the picture window, I savored the beauty of the rhododendron, now in full bloom. Its large pink blossoms blended in beautifully with the deep green of the evergreen trees, and I thought, *Maybe this is why I always tend to decorate in tones of pink and green.*

I always felt loved and secure in this little room right next to Mother and Daddy's larger one. The bed was the same. Yes, the same bed where many years ago I lay sick. I was only four years old. I was ill, so ill that Mother was worried even though my doctor grandfather lived just across the street. She watched me closely, coming in and out of my room to bring me cool drinks and to stroke my fevered brow.

Toward afternoon, when my fever climbed even higher, Mother sat on the edge of my bed and began to talk to me about heaven. She asked me if I wanted to go there.

"Of course," I said.

She repeated one of my favorite stories, the story of God sending

His beloved Son, Jesus, to die on the cross for me. She explained simply how God loved me and wanted me in heaven with Him when I died, but because of my sin and badness I couldn't go. But God sent Jesus to die as punishment for my sins. She quoted John 3:16, placing my name in the verse. "For God so loved Gigi, that He gave His only beloved Son, so that if Gigi believes in Him Gigi will not perish but have eternal life."

She also told me an amazing thing. She said if I had been the only little girl in the whole world, Jesus would still have come and died for me. She asked me if I understood. Of course I didn't understand it all, but I knew I was often bad and needed help to be good. I knew I wanted to go to heaven when I died, so when Mother asked me if I wanted to ask Jesus into my heart to take away my badness, I said yes. I simply bowed my head and opened my heart to Jesus.

I don't actually remember this day, but I've heard the story so many times I can easily relive the experience. At the age of four, I certainly didn't understand the theological implications of my simple decision to say yes to Jesus, but I knew it was real. It was a beginning. And Paul assures us that "he who began a good work in you will carry it on to completion" (Philippians 1:6).

Not long ago I was contemplating all my material blessings and the fact that I couldn't take any of them to heaven with me: not my favorite trunk from China nor my precious pictures and irreplaceable letters. Suddenly it occurred to me that all I really *can* take to heaven are my children (or other souls I've led to the Savior). What a wonderful, blessed thought—but also what an awesome responsibility.

When our eldest son was only three, he was sitting beside his daddy on the balcony of our home in Switzerland, enjoying the view. Suddenly he asked, "Daddy, how can I ask Jesus into my heart?"

Stephan was surprised but took him seriously and discovered he was really ready. That day our eldest became a child of God, and he has never wavered.

Years later, as a teenager, this son was putting his youngest sister, Jerushah, to bed. As he tucked her in, he quoted the verse, "Behold, I stand at the door, and knock: if any man hear my voice, and open the door, I will come in" (Revelation 3:20 KJV). He explained that this was Jesus knocking at the door of her life; then he asked if she would like Him to come in and live with her. She said yes and then prayed to receive Christ.

Jerushah has never forgotten that night. She didn't understand everything, but for her, too, this was the beginning.

A young divinity student once asked Dr. Karl Barth, the great Swiss theologian, what was the one greatest theological truth. The young man, expecting a long dissertation, sat down. Dr. Barth stood and walked to the podium. "The greatest theological truth I know," he said, "Is 'Jesus loves me, this I know, for the Bible tells me so.'" And with that, Dr. Barth sat down.

This is a theology that even little children can comprehend. It is never too early to begin teaching this to our children, nor is it ever too late. Yes, it may be more difficult when they are teenagers or older, but God can touch a heart at any age.

And I hope that He has touched *your* heart as we've shared these glimpses into His truth. If He has, I want to encourage you to make sure of your own relationship with Jesus Christ. Have you ever opened your heart and life to Him? If not, there may never be a better time than right now.

It's very simple. Just pause right now, wherever you are, and say to the Lord words similar to the ones below. He will hear you!

Lord Jesus, thank You for dying on the cross for me. Please forgive me of all my sins and come into my life right now as my Savior and Lord. Thank You for making it possible to one day go to heaven and share eternity with You. Amen.

If you already know the Lord, let me encourage you to take the spiritual questions of your children very seriously. Be prepared to explain in simple terms how they, too, can ask Jesus into their hearts.

Remember, you can bring nothing with you into heaven except those you have brought to Jesus.

See you there, if not before!

A Final Thought

～

There is one thing certain about life: it never stands still.

Every summer I spend several weeks at my childhood home. The little stream is still there, flowing faithfully along. It keeps moving, day after day, month after month. It gurgles during the spring thaws. It thrives during the summer storms. It meanders around the hurdles of fall. It continues to flow even under the ice of winter, on its constant course to the river down the valley...and on to the sea.

During those serene summer days, I sit on the terrace, watching the younger members of the family play with my grandchildren in this same little stream where I played. As I do, I am reminded just how fast my life is passing.

Time hastens on, and eternity lies ahead.

Through the swift course of our days, there are many opportunities to make a difference, to touch our families, our communities, and our world. Those differences may seem small on the surface, but in the eternal scheme of things, who can tell? But these opportunities are rushing by, never to be retrieved.

How needful I am of God's wisdom and strength. How much I need those jewel-like insights that flash like chunks of mica from a stream in the early morning sunlight. And I have discovered that they are there for the finding.

Proverbs 2:6 (NKJV) tells us that:

The LORD gives wisdom;
From His mouth come knowledge and understanding.

He is the source, the fountain of living water…from Him flows strength, wisdom, joy, peace like a river, and all the treasures of wisdom and knowledge (Isaiah 66:12; Jeremiah 2:13; Colossians 2:3).

I would have never found those shining stones (and rubies) in the little mountain stream if I hadn't spent hours looking. In the same way, we will find all we need in Him and in His Word as we walk hour by hour, minute by minute beside our Lord.

I have often failed to rely on the Lord for that needed wisdom and strength. I don't want to miss out on any more, and I trust you don't either.

We need wisdom and strength to keep us on the right path.

Wisdom and strength to sustain and comfort us in moments of crisis, stress, and sorrow.

Wisdom to help us lead and direct those lives God positions along our path.

Psalm 1 tells us that if we walk with the Lord, we shall be like trees planted by rivers of water, that bring forth fruit in season. Like those trees, our leaves will never dry up and wither, and whatever we do will prosper.

But we need to stay planted near the stream, allowing our roots to run deep. And if we follow on to know the Lord, He promises to lead us beside still, quiet waters.

May His life flowing through you produce all the strength, beauty, and refreshment that you will ever need.

Some people call that "the Christian life."

I call it, *Currents of the Heart*.

NOTES

Chapter One: Imaginations

1. See 2 Corinthians 10:5.

Chapter Eight: A Blessing from the Birds

1. Elizabeth Cheney, "Overheard in an Orchard," in *The Best Loved Religious Poems* (Old Tappan, N.J.: Fleming H. Revell, 1933, renewed 1961), 215.

2. Adapted from Mrs. C. D. Martin, "His Eye Is on the Sparrow," in *Select Church Songs* (Dallas: Stamps-Baxter Music/Zondervan, 1965).

Chapter Nine. Where Are the Front Lines?

1. Armelle Nicolas, 1606-71, quoted in Mary Wilder Tileston, comp., *Joy and Strength* (New York: Grosset and Dunlap Publishers by arrangement with Little, Brown, and Co., 1986).

2. A sweet-smelling sacrifice typifies affectionate devotion to the Father's will. See notes on Leviticus 1:9 in *Oxford NIV Scofield Study Bible* (New York: Oxford University Press, 1967).

Chapter Ten: A Vision of Forgiveness

1. Haldor Lillenas, "Wonderful Grace of Jesus," copyright 1918, renewed 1946. Assigned to Hope Publishing Company, Carol Stream, Ill.

Chapter Eleven: The Concert

1. Doris Akers, "Sweet, Sweet Spirit" (Burbank, Calif.: Manna Music, 1962).

Chapter Thirteen: God's 9-1-1 Line

1. F. B. Meyer, *Ephesians: A Devotional Commentary* (n.p.: Marshall Morgan and Scott, n.d.), 12.

Chapter Twenty: Unwelcome News

1. Described in the chapter entitled "Hope," in Gigi Tchividjian's earlier book, *Weather of the Heart,* 97-101.

Chapter Twenty-four: The Keeper

1. Named for Tertullian, the church father. I was studying church history while I carried this child and prayed, "Lord, if you give me a son, please give him a mind like Tertullian's so he will always defend the gospel of Jesus Christ."